DOUBLE LIFE

To Pauline
with love and all
best wishes,

DOUBLE LIFE

John Freestone

The Book Guild Ltd
Sussex, England

The Book Guild Ltd
25 High Street,
Lewes, Sussex

First published 1998
© John Freestone 1998
Set in Times
Typesetting by Wordset,
Lewes, East Sussex

Printed in Great Britain by
Bookcraft (Bath) Ltd,
Avon

A catalogue record for this book is
available from the British Library

ISBN 1 85776 345 9

CONTENTS

PREFACE

I have called this little book 'Double Life' for the very obvious reaon that I spent a happy and I hope successful career as a teacher, culminating in twenty years as the headmaster of a large primary school, and at the same time I occupied all my spare moments with my musical activities, giving recitals as a tenor and studying singing with three eminent teachers, Blanche Marchesi, Walter Hyde and Maggie Teyte. My initial studies with Blanche Marchesi were sufficiently encouraging to make me think of making music my career, but this ambition was quickly dispelled when I was called up in 1940 and served five years in the Royal Artillery. When I was finally 'demobbed' in September 1945 it was obviously too late for me to make a fresh start as a professional tenor, and I returned to teaching quite happily.

I was now 35 and was quickly engaged in the evenings with playing the tenor lead in a number of Gilbert and Sullivan operas in East Grinstead, Lewes and Brighton. However, when I was 40 I thought it was time to stop playing the tenor roles which were always the juvenile lead but I continued to sing at concerts and as soloist with local choral societies, and I started to produce the operas for the Burgess Hill Operatic Society and I also resolved to start giving singing lessons. In other words it meant that I was leading a double life as school teacher and professional musician.

When I retired in 1971 music dominated my life and I did not suffer, as many people do on first retiring, wondering how to occupy my time. In addition to my active interest in music I started giving many talks to local societies and also began writing for *The Gramophone* as a music critic and continued a little later in the same capacity for *Hi-Fi News and Record Review*.

My interest in singing and vocal technique brought another offshoot into my life. I started collecting recordings of the great singers of the past and I was enthralled to hear some of the discs of

Caruso, De Lucia, Tamagno, Melba, Patti, Tetrazzini and other world famous artists. As I have mentioned my collecting at some length in the book, I feel that it is necessary to explain as briefly as possible some of the terms in common use by collectors of early vocal records.

The main record companies in the first decade of this century were The Gramophone Company, Columbia, Fonotipia, Odeon and the International Zonophone Company. The first celebrity records were those issued by the Gramophone and Typewriter Company (later the Gramophone Company and His Master's Voice), and they were recorded in Russia in 1901 and were issued with red and gold labels. They are known among collectors as 'Red G&Ts' and are fabulously rare. These were followed in 1902 by similar discs (all single sided) by Caruso and a little later by Melba, Patti, and Albani. In 1906 the word 'typewriter' was omitted from the labels and these discs are known as 'Pre-dogs' because the dog trademark was not yet used. This was introduced in 1909 and a year later the trade name 'His Master's Voice' appeared.

The International Zonophone Company was largely an Italian concern and many famous artists recorded for them, including Caruso. They were all single sided with either a light blue or orange label, but the company only lasted until 1905, when they were bought out by the Gramophone Company and further issues were relegated to cheap recordings by lesser artists.

The Columbia Company made an early effort to rival the Gramophone Company, when they released some celebrity records in 1903, but the former, in conjunction with their American partners, the Victor Company, had already obtained exclusive contracts with most of the well known singers of the period, and for some years Columbia concentrated their efforts on issuing popular recordings at lower prices.

The Fonotipia and Odeon companies were mainly occupied in recording Italian and German artists who were famous on the continent but less well known in Great Britain and the United States.

I am now in my 88th year, and my many friends have persuaded me to write this autobiography, which I hope will be of some interest. I am very fortunate in that my old friend and former pupil Donald (now Sir Donald) Sinden had agreed to write a foreword, and I send him my warmest thanks for his kindness and interest.

FOREWORD

The recently acquired jackboots of Hitler, Mussolini and Franco were beginning to echo in the streets of Europe. In England a tunnel linking Liverpool with Birkenhead was opened by King George V and Queen Mary, and the whole country rejoiced as they celebrated the 25th anniversary of the king's accession to the throne. Every village was *en fête*: streets were adorned with flags and garlands and each shop window carried a display of silver crowns and photographs of Their Majesties tinselled and beribboned in red, white and blue. In London the adored monarch rode in the famous gilded Coronation Coach from Buckingham Palace to a service in St Paul's Cathedral. The year was 1935.

But in Sussex, in the village of Ditchling, in a house in the High Street little could alleviate the gloom. The eldest son of Mr and Mrs Sinden had failed his eleven-plus examination.

I – for it was I who had failed the eleven-plus – was a rather sickly child who suffered from asthma and perforce had missed many – too many – days from Junior School, so instead of going to a Grammar or Secondary Modern School as my cousin had, and my brother was later to do, I would have to go to the nearest State Senior School for the next four years. This would involve cycling a mile and a half to Hassocks station, a train journey to Burgess Hill and a walk of two hundred yards down the hill.

The headmaster was a large, feared man by the name of Woolcock. Pupils lived in dread of being sent to his room for the customary swish of the cane – but we knew that if that should happen, the fault was ours. We had broken the rules. The choice was ours, I was no good at games – the asthma again – and I was bullied by the 'hearties'. Perhaps sensing this I was taken under the wing of one of the most remarkable men I have ever known. His name was John Freestone and he changed my life.

'Mr Freestone' showed me that there were finer things in life than football and *Comic Cuts* or *The Wizard*. He 'opened doors' and helped me to appreciate all things artistic – good literature, good music, good paintings. I soon discovered that he was a singer of considerable talent – but I will let him tell you about that – and regularly sang in Gilbert and Sullivan at his old school, the Brighton and Hove Grammar. I well remember hearing him as Nanki Poo in *The Mikado*. On one memorable occasion he told me that he was going to a recital in the nearby village of Lindfield (or was it Haywards Heath?) to hear a tenor who was becoming well known, accompanied on the piano by his friend who was the composer of some of the songs. Would I like to join him? Off we went and heard the first performance of *Seven Sonnets of Michelangelo* set to music by Benjamin Britten who also played the piano while they were sung by Peter Pears. This was the beginning of my love/hate relationship with Britten.

Thus began a friendship with John – or Jack as we call him – that has lasted more than 60 years. Now let him tell you the story of his life in his own way.

Sir Donald Sinden.
February 1998

1

A Musical Legacy

I was born 23 July 1910 in Haywards Heath, a small market town in Mid Sussex. It owed its existence to the fact that when the London to Brighton railway was constructed, the citizens of Cuckfield had refused to allow it to pass through their neighbourhood, so a détour was made, and a station was built at Haywards Heath which was a tiny hamlet of no importance.

At about this time my paternal great grandfather Richard Pannet realized that Haywards Heath and its railway station would soon grow in importance, and he moved from Lewes and opened a builder's business in Haywards Heath. His foresight proved profitable and he became the founder of a very lucrative undertaking. In the meantime he had married, and his son Arthur Pannet was born in Bulltrough Farm, on the corner of Boltro Road.

Arthur Pannet was brought up in his father's business and studied to become an architect and when the time came he quickly established himself in that profession and was responsible for designing most of the buildings which the Haywards Heath Council required. He married and had two daughters. The elder Genevieve married a local schoolmaster, Owen Freestone. They in turn had three sons, my older brother Dick, who later had a distinguished career in the Air Force, Harold who died in infancy, and finally myself. My mother's sister, Evangeline, eventually married the son of a Brighton publican and moved to Brighton.

By this time Haywards Heath was a small market town in which everyone knew everyone else, and there were certain well

1

known local characters who might well have walked straight out of the pages of a Dickens novel or Hardy's *Under the Greenwood Tree*. There was a prosperous butcher who proudly displayed on a board outside his shop the following rather ambiguous advertisement, 'Try my sausages – they are unapproachable'. Then there was a local milliner who claimed that he made regular visits to Paris to bring back the latest Parisian creations and he greeted his customers with 'These are the very latest French models, madam – very rekerkee', which was as near as he could get to Recherché. Then there was a strange individual always referred to as 'Fiddle Botting' who earned a precarious living as the local 'rag and bone man'. He had a curious loping walk and this was supposed to have been caused by his mother having been frightened by a performing bear when she was carrying him. Then there was an old lady named Mrs French who was almost a reincarnation of Mrs Gamp. She always wore a black bonnet and was swathed in several layers of voluminous black skirts. She had a certain local reputation for her knowledge of herbs, which she used for medicinal purposes, and she made her own pills which she sold to the local townsfolk, claiming that their efficacy was greatly enhanced because she always sang hymns reverently as she made them.

This was the Haywards Heath into which I was born just before the First World War and in which I was brought up. Travel was difficult as motor cars were very few, and a favourite means of transport for those who could afford it was the local horse-drawn carriage. A visit to Brighton – a mere 15 miles away – was considered by the local inhabitants as a major undertaking. I still remember that when I was very young and the family went on our annual holiday in August, we were taken to Haywards Heath station in a horse drawn cab, which seemed to me the very height of luxury.

At home we had to make our own entertainment as there was no radio or television and gramophones and phonographs were luxuries few could afford. A piano, on the other hand, was to be found in all but the very poorest of houses, and we made our own music as best we could. My earliest memories are of my mother singing sentimental Victorian ballads in her very beautiful mezzo-soprano voice.

She had studied singing at the Brighton School of Music under the principal, Lyall Taylor, and vividly remembered the occasion when the famous conductor, Luigi Arditi, came down to Brighton to adjudicate and distribute prizes at the music school. Taylor was quite merciless in his criticisms and said to Arditi, while pointing to my mother, 'This girl has the best voice in the school, but she will never make a singer. She has no soul'. Actually she told me that she was petrified with fear whenever she was asked to sing in public and after appearing at a few local concerts she gladly gave up the struggle.

Taylor was probably right in his assessment of my mother's musicianship. She liked sentimental ballads and freely admitted that the classics as a whole bored her. She preferred Bucalossi's 'Grasshopper's Dance' to Beethoven's 'Moonlight Sonata' and at a rather pretentious party given by a local hostess she shocked the assembled guests, who had all spoken of their love of classical music, by saying that her favourite composer was Sousa!

Her father had taken her, when she was 17, to hear the celebrated soprano Adelina Patti, but she was not impressed. She found Patti altogether too stiff and formal in her tight-fitting stomacher encrusted with diamonds, and preferred the darling of the music halls, Marie Lloyd, who came over as a warm personality, although the latter's vulgarities rather shocked her.

My father was a much more serious musician. He was the headmaster of a local state school in Haywards Heath. He had been a student at King Alfred's College, Winchester, and when Sir John Stainer, who was the chief inspector of music for schools, came down to the college, my father, who had a light but serviceable tenor voice was chosen to sing the tenor solos in 'The Crucifixion' in the presence of the composer. He was congratulated by Sir John, but his main interest was in playing the organ or the piano.

One of my earliest memories is of his performing a piano arrangement of the overture to Wagner's *Tannhaüser*, and this fascinated me. For some weeks I pestered my father to give a daily repeat performance! About this time I developed a promising treble voice and as we had to make our own musical entertainment in those days I began to take an interest in music.

3

We often had musical evenings at which my mother and I sang and my father played selections from the 'Star Folio' – a well known collection of piano pieces – to which we all listened rapturously.

With the end of the First World War in 1918, things gradually returned to normal, and there were occasional concerts given in Haywards Heath with local artists performing their party pieces. I enjoyed these immensely but longed to hear the famous singers whose names I frequently heard and who came to Brighton from time to time.

I had an older brother named Richard (Dick) who had obtained a scholarship from the local school to Brighton and Hove Grammar School and it was hoped that I would follow him there. Fortunately I passed the necessary tests and so in 1921 I started to go to school in Brighton.

During the next few years I was mainly occupied with my school studies but fortunately for me we were given a short gramophone recital after morning assembly every Friday, and it was there that I first heard recordings of some of the greatest artists of the day. I was thrilled by the sound of Caruso's voice and a little later I heard a record of the great soprano Amelita Galli Curci singing the 'Air and Variations' by Proch and I had never in my wildest dreams thought that a human voice could sing with such ease and brilliance. This sealed my fate. I had to have a gramophone, for the human voice was, and still is, the great love of my life.

Apart from the weekly gramophone recitals, my school life passed fairly uneventfully from a musical point of view, with one or two notable exceptions. One was a broadcast by the great Italian diva, Luisa Tetrazzini on 10 March 1925. This was promoted with tremendous publicity by the *Evening Standard*, and other artists who took part in the concert were the violinist Isolde Menges, the pianist Frederic Lamond, the contralto Phyllis Lett, the baritones Dinh Gilly and John Goss, the cellist W.H. Squire and the Kedroff Quartette. Tetrazzini sang 'O luce di quest anima' from Donizetti's *Linda di Chamounix,* 'L'Altra notte' from Boito's *Mefistofele* and 'Un bel di vedremo' from Puccini's *Madama Butterfly* as well as some songs, finishing with 'The last rose of summer' in her own delightful brand of English. Her accompanist was Ivor Newton and I listened to the concert on my recently-acquired crystal set, having bought a new 'Cat's whisker' for the occasion. I did not of course realize that Tetrazzini was much past her best but I listened enthralled to the still amazing voice of the great singer.

In 1926 I upgraded my equipment to a valve detector and a two-valve amplifier plus a loud speaker with a small trumpet. In 1926 too there was the broadcast of Melba's farewell from Covent Garden and this was of course another red letter day for me. I was barely 16 and had no knowledge of operatic works, but I recall being entranced by the crystal purity of Melba's voice even at that late stage of her career.

Still later in 1926 I was taken, together with a school friend, to hear Dame Clara Butt at the Dome in Brighton, and this was the very first occasion on which I heard a celebrated singer in the flesh! Dame Clara had a most striking stage presence. I imagine she must have been at least six feet tall and she was dressed from head to foot in gold lamé with a short train and bandeau and shoes to match. She had made her first professional appearance in a performance of Sullivan's *Gold Legend* in 1892 when only 19 and was an immediate and overwhelming success. Although she had been singing for 34 years when I heard her, and her voice was showing signs of wear, it was still a phenomenal instrument of immense power and wide range. I remember she sang 'Abide with me' written especially for her by her accompanist Samuel Liddle, 'Land of Hope and Glory' and 'The Lost Chord' in which she completely eclipsed the Dome organ which was itself capable of considerable volume.

Much has been written about Dame Clara and there is no doubt that hers was a unique voice. She could sing sublimely when she was interpreting the old masters. Her recordings of 'Lusinghe più care' from Handel's *Alessandro* and 'Rendi'l sereno al ciglio' from Handel's *Sosarme* are gramophone classics with no trace of the break between the chest and medium registers which later became noticeable. Her coloratura technique was amazing with a beautifully controlled trill on some of her earliest discs. She had a voice and appearance which cried out for an operatic career, but

5

apart from some student performances in Gluck's *Orfeo ed Euridice* and a few appearances in the same opera at Covent Garden in the 1920s she devoted most of her time to concert work and oratorio. Elgar was a great admirer of her voice and artistry and wrote his 'Sea Pictures' especially for her and he described her as his 'Ideal Angel' in *The Dream of Gerontius*. The tragedy was that she spent so much of her time singing sentimental second-rate ballads which were quite unworthy of her unique talents. When Melba first heard that Dame Clara was giving a concert tour in Australia she apparently told her to 'Sing them muck', but as Ivor Newton remarked, such advice was unnecessary!

The end of 1926 created more musical excitement for me. Every year at the end of the Christmas term, Brighton and Hove Grammar School put on, for a whole week, one of the Gilbert and Sullivan operas, and all the boys were given an audition to see if they had any potential as singers. By this time my voice had descended, it never broke, and I was now a tenor! Dr Hector, the senior music master, told me that he thought I had the makings of a good voice and placed me in the chorus for the production of *Ruddigore* with the promise of a principal part if I was still at the school the following year. Rehearsals for the opera were a marvellous experience for me and during the week of the show I lived in a musical dreamland. A sense of emptiness and boredom followed, as I came down to earth with a bump, but the Christmas holidays soon helped to restore me to something like normality.

The year 1927 started with the prospect of examinations in June and July and my time was fully occupied with school work. I was fortunate enough to do sufficiently well in the old Senior Cambridge examinations to be excused matriculation, but now my future had to be carefully considered. My headmaster, Mr Barron, suggested that I might stay at school for a further year with a view to going on to university, but my parents wanted me to become a bank clerk. I was quite happy to follow their wishes, and so, later in the autumn of 1927, I became a very junior clerk in Barclay's bank in the branch near St Peter's Church in London Road, Brighton.

I spent a rather unhappy year in the bank. I soon realized that I

6

was not suited to the rather restricted life I had to live. As this was just before the first calculating machines were introduced, my day consisted largely of adding up long columns of figures and addressing endless envelopes for the bank's customers. On one occasion I sent out the month's statements to the bank's clients without sealing the envelopes, and the manager, Mr Hough, who was the most understanding and gentle of men, was, not unnaturally, a little annoyed! At the end of my first year I was given six months' probation, and this decided me. I handed in my resignation. I had, of course, discussed this with my parents and it was suggested that I should become a teacher. For a year I worked as an uncertificated student teacher at my father's school, and then went on to King Alfred's College, Winchester, where my father had also received his training.

During the time which elapsed before I went to Winchester, I had the opportunity to go to some concerts at the Dome in Brighton and I was fortunate enough to hear two of the artists whose records I greatly admired. The first was Count John McCormack who came to the Dome in 1929. The great tenor had made his début at Covent Garden in 1907 and for some years he sang in opera, particularly in America, but following the First World War his performances in opera were few and he eventually confined himself to singing in concerts, where he felt more at home. Naturally by 1929 his voice was not what it had once been, and initially I was rather disappointed when I first heard him. His voice was smaller than his wonderful early records had given me to believe, and although there was a lovely sympathetic quality, the ringing top notes were no longer in evidence. After performing a selection of classical songs, John devoted much of the programme to English art songs and popular Irish ballads in which he was inimitable. I remember he always carried a little book of words with him, but I cannot recall that he ever opened it. As the concert progressed, his artistry and utter sincerity soon captivated us all. I remember particularly his wonderful singing of Ford's 'Since first I saw your face I resolved to honour and renown you', given with such simplicity that it went straight to the heart. The voice may not have been as fine as when he was in his prime, but his wonderful diction and phrasing, and his ability

7

to suggest that he was improvising the songs as he went along were unique.

John also had a great sense of humour. He told a friend of mine that the superb French bass, Pol Plançon was gay, saying 'The poor man couldn't rehearse if there was a good looking boy in the theatre. He was ambisextrous!'

The next concert which I had eagerly anticipated was given by one of my great favourites, Amelita Galli-Curci. By this time I had acquired quite a few of her records, and loved them, and again I was a little disappointed. Like McCormack she was a little past her best by 1929, having made her début in Italy in 1906, and she was suffering from goitre which must have affected her singing. However, her voice, though small, was of a uniquely beautiful quality, and the charm of her singing soon delighted her audience. The very highest notes now lacked the easy brilliance shown in her recordings, but when she sang 'Lo here the gentle lark' and other show pieces she captivated her listeners. She amused us all before singing an aria from Meyerbeer's *L'Etoile du nord*. This should have been accompanied by two flautists but madam apologized for the absence of one of them by announcing in her delightful broken English 'I am sorry, I have only one flute. The other has caught a cold!'

Galli-Curci gave some final concerts in England in 1934 and I heard her again in the Dome, when she still sang beautifully, but it was obvious that she was near the end of her great career. In 1935 she had an operation to remove a large goitre and although she made a few appearances until 1937, she never regained complete control of her voice, and wisely retired.

By 1929 my voice had now settled down into that of a respectable tenor and I was invited to sing at a concert in Haywards Heath before I had had any voice training. The song I chose was 'Passing by' by Edward C. Purcell – not the great Purcell – but the composer of some pleasing ballads. No one seemed in the least impressed, but I practised at home and determined to have singing lessons when I could afford them.

In the meantime I was looking forward eagerly to going to college in Winchester. King Alfred's College was a Church of England establishment, and both the principal, Canon Wainright, and the vice principal, were clergymen. Conditions were decidedly spartan for young men who had been accustomed to an easy life at home. First year students were accommodated in a long unheated dormitory, divided into cubicles each containing a small bed and a chest of drawers. We were awakened at 6.30 am by the ringing of a bell, aptly named 'the first tinkle', and we were expected to have completed our toilet in time for the first lecture of the day at 7 am. Breakfast followed at 8 am after which we all went to the college chapel for morning prayers. These were followed by a short break and then from 9 am we attended further lectures until 1 pm, with a short break for coffee at 11 am.

After lunch the rest of the day was free, but of course we were expected to occupy our time with private study. Supper was served at 7 pm and lights out followed at 10 pm. Recreation consisted of football in the winter, cricket and tennis in the summer, and in addition there was a large common room where billiards, snooker and table tennis could be played.

We were given music lessons by a baritone who was a soloist in the choir of Winchester Cathedral and eventually I had my first singing lessons from him. I remember that we concentrated on scales and solfeggi for a few months and then I was told to study and prepare the opening tenor solos from Handel's *Messiah* – the recitative 'Comfort ye' and the air 'Every valley shall be exalted'. I made little progress however and apart from singing solos at one or two concerts in the college, my only musical activities were centred round the college choir. A great occasion which I remember well was when we joined forces with other local choirs and took part in the very first performance of Dr George Dyson's *Canterbury Pilgrims* in 1931. The part of the Wife of Bath was taken by a young soprano called Bella Baillie, who later became famous as Isobel Baillie. Her voice was ideal for the part and she later recorded the solo 'A good wyf was ther of bisyde Bathe'. Dr Dyson was the principal music master at Winchester School at that time and the famous school was well known for its music excellence, largely due to the talent and enthusiasm of its teachers. Dr Dyson himself was well known as one of the leading composers of his day and he was instrumental in bringing many famous artists to the town, including Dr Malcolm Sargent, Stuart

9

Wilson, Astra Desmond, Keith Falkner and Roy Henderson, while works given during my three years at the college included Handel's *Messiah* and Bach's *Mass in B Minor*.

I stayed on at college for a third year, having obtained my teacher's certificate at the conclusion of the two year course, and concentrated my efforts on working for an honours degree in French, and spending a summer vacation in the lovely city of Tours.

Life in Tours in the early 1930s was quite unlike anything I had previously experienced. I was still very innocent and I remember sitting alone in a café in the French city and a woman who seemed middle-aged to me – she was probably about 30 – winked as she passed by my table. I was rather surprised and took no notice. Later the same evening I was talking to a French gentleman who was helping me with my French studies and I asked him if a woman could go alone to a café in Tours. His reply was terse and to the point. He said, 'Si vous voyez une femme seule dans un café vous pouvez lui demander de coucher avec elle' ('If you see a woman alone in a café, you can ask her to go to bed with you'.) In other words no respectable woman could go unaccompanied to a café in France. How times have changed!

My third year at college went all too quickly and then I obtained a teaching post as assistant master in Junction Road School, Burgess Hill. This was only two miles from Haywards Heath and so I was able to live at home. However the conditions under which I started teaching were very difficult. I had to share a large classroom with the headmaster, who taught the older children at one end of the room, while I taught the 11 and 12 year old age group at the other end! My inexperience was all too obvious and the headmaster did little to help me and frequently interrupted, when he felt that I was not controlling my class in the very rigid way that he required. The result was that I became over anxious and was really too tired to think of singing in the evenings. However as the year progressed, I eventually met an old American gentleman who lived in a large house in Vicarage Gardens, Brighton. He had studied with the famous Monsieur Wartel who lived in Paris and who had a great reputation as a singing teacher and whose pupils included the famous Swedish soprano Christine Nilsson. His name was Richard Ball Dodson and he was already in his nineties. He lived for many years in Paris and had heard the premières of *Lakmé* and *Manon*. He gave me a good technical grounding and refused to take any payment, and then suggested that I should study with an operatic soprano who had retired and was now living in Brighton.

Her name was Marguerite Anderson and she had sung with the British National Opera Company and was the Manon in the company's performances of the Massenet work opposite the Des Grieux of Heddle Nash.

School finished for the week on Friday afternoon and so I was able to go for my weekly singing lesson on Saturday mornings, when my voice was less tired. Under the rather difficult conditions I still managed to make good progress and Madam Anderson kept me on exercises, including scales and solfeggi for a full year. She then suggested that I should enter for the tenor championship in the Brighton Competitive Musical Festival, and I was very happy to do so.

There were four classes for tenors, one for lyrical and one for dramatic songs, plus set pieces from oratorio and opera. At my first attempt I came first in the operatic class, singing in English Siegmund's Liebeslied from Wagner's *Die Walküre*, but I was beaten by a small margin in the aggregate marks for the four classes. The adjudicator was the well known baritone and teacher Roy Henderson. Among his remarks and criticisms he wrote, 'But the promise of the voice is so good that further study will be well worthwhile'. I was naturally encouraged by this and for the next three years I entered the festival, winning the tenor championship each time. I then felt that further entry would be pointless but as a result of my successes, and the publicity given in the local newspapers, I obtained a number of small professional engagements. One that I particularly liked was singing the role of Raleigh in Edward German's *Merrie England*, with local societies in Sussex.

At about the same time I was offered the role of Ralph Rackstraw in *HMS Pinafore* with the Lindfield Operatic Society, and I stayed with them as principal tenor until 1940 when I was conscripted into the army. In 1936 I also sang the role of Nanki

11

Poo in *The Mikado* with the Lewes Operatic Society, and I was also happy to go back to Brighton and Hove Grammar School as an old boy to help them with their Christmas shows, including the tenor leads in the Gilbert and Sullivan operas.

Now that I was earning a modest salary as a teacher I was able to make occasional visits to London, and I started going to Covent Garden. I had already heard glowing reports of a new coloratura soprano, Lily Pons, and I booked a seat in the amphitheatre at Covent Garden to hear her sing Rosina in *Il Barbiere di Siviglia* on 31 May 1935. I was delighted, when I arrived at the theatre, to find that the great Italian baritone Guiseppe de Luca was to make an unheralded appearance as Figaro in a cast which also included Dino Borgioli as Count Almaviva and the magnificent bass Ezio Pinza as Don Basilio. The evening went splendidly. Lily Pons sang brilliantly and acted charmingly as Rosina and De Luca was a superbly polished Figaro, singing with an ease and freedom which belied his years.

Many record collectors who have only heard the later discs of Lily Pons are inclined to dismiss her as a second rate coloratura, but in the late twenties when she made her Odeon records and in the early 1930s when she recorded for Victor, she proved herself a charming artist with a well produced voice of good quality extending to a full toned F in Alt. Her later discs, made for Columbia with an orchestral accompaniment by her husband, André Kostelanetz, are very inferior both artistically and technically.

Later in the same year I went to Convent Garden to hear *Un Ballo in Maschera* by Verdi. The cast included Eva Turner as Amelia, Stella Andreva as Oscar, Constance Willis as Ulrica, Dino Borgioli as Ricardo and Arthur Fear as Renato. I had heard Dame Eva on some Columbia records which I possessed, but though excellent they gave me no idea of the impact her singing would make in the theatre. Her aria 'Ma dall 'arido stelo divulsa' was the most thrilling singing I have ever experienced. She sang with tremendous dramatic intensity and with such volume in the big climaxes that the auditorium was flooded with glowing tone. I was sitting next to an Italian who turned to me and said 'And they say the English cannot sing. Dio mio!' At that time Eva Turner was just a distant luminary and I did not dream for one moment that many years later she would become a very dear friend at whose villa on Lake Lugano I was to spend my summer holidays for a number of years, but that is something which belongs to post–war times and will be recalled later.

2

Early Career: The Unwilling Soldier

At this time I suppose I still had hopes of becoming a full time professional singer, but there were many difficulties in the way. My father had recently retired on a small pension and it would have been impossible for him to have financed me until I was established. I also realized that despite Roy Henderson's encouraging remarks about my voice I was still having many technical problems. After a concert at the Grand Hotel in Brighton I found that my throat was aching for several days. I had certainly sung a tiring programme including 'E lucevan le stelle' from Puccini's *Tosca* and 'How vain is man' from Handel's *Judas Maccabaeus* and then I joined my teacher, Marguerite Anderson, in the love duet from the first act of Puccini's *Madama Butterfly*, but I felt that there was something seriously wrong with the way I was producing my voice. A little later Madam Anderson asked me to prepare the music of the whole of the Garden Scene from Gounod's *Faust* which included the aria 'Salut demeure chaste et pure' (All hail thou dwelling pure and lowly), rising to a high C at the climax. I again found the music too taxing for me. I was only 27, and at last I decided that I must make a drastic change and find a new teacher. I heard that Blanche Marchesi was living in London and was giving lessons at her home at 78 Lancaster Gate. I wrote to her asking for an audition and had a reply stating that she would be pleased to receive me on a Saturday afternoon.

My first meeting with the famous singer and teacher was, for me, an unforgettable experience. Blanche had met at her mother's studio in Paris many of the legendary figures in the world of music including Liszt, Gounod, Saint-Saens, Massenet and of course Nellie Melba and Emma Eames who had been her mother's pupils.

On being ushered into her large studio by her maid Zenia, I felt the keen scrutiny of a pair of eyes, sharp and clear and ageless, and then, as I approached, the eyes softened and an old but cultured voice invited me to sit down. For the moment I relaxed and took note of my surroundings and of Blanche herself. She was old and physically weak but her character held an almost superhuman strength. Her face, while not beautiful by ordinary standards, had a dignity, a refinement, and a searching intelligence, with its clear-cut features and wisps of white hair. Her pallor was such that one was reminded of the sculpture of legend brought to life by the artist's touch.

Another pupil was still having a lesson and so I was able to take stock of my surroundings. First I noticed the famous bust of Blanche's mother, Mathilde Marchesi, presented to her by Mary Mintoff, an American pupil who had a highly successful career as a concert singer in Germany. Then, above this was a portrait of Blanche herself as a younger woman, while the walls were covered with sketches and prints and paintings, many of them typically Victorian in design and execution. The piano was covered with autographed photos of many famous artists and personalities from all walks of life. Many of the names have slipped my memory but one, a signed photograph of Kaiser Wilhelm remains clear in my mind. There was a careless profusion of furniture, rather fragile looking Louis Seize chairs predominating, but the general effect was pleasing and entirely right for Blanche's personality. It was a room full of memories of the past, and what a glorious past it suggested!

My thoughts were brought sharply back to the present by the departure of the pupil who had been singing. Extreme nervousness combined with the importance (to me!) of the occasion have almost erased most memories of that *first lesson*, but I do remember that Blanche questioned me closely as to how I breathed and appeared satisfied that I was using what is generally called the 'lateral costal' method of breathing in which the diaphragm is pulled in to support the raised lungs. Caruso used this method and said of it in his quaint English, 'When I sing, my

15

stomach and my bottom seem to come together'. Blanche then asked me to sing a scale and an arpeggio and finally an aria. She then said, 'You have a voice of good quality, but your method is all wrong and the voice would soon have been ruined, but I will restore it.'

As the months progressed I began to realize more and more that Blanche Marchesi was no mere singing teacher. She was a great personality, a most generous friend and an extremely discerning critic. Her genius as an interpretative artist transcended anything I had previously heard. On one occasion I was learning Schubert's 'Erlkönig' and Blanche, whose voice, following a stroke, had all but disappeared, half sang and half whispered this great song in such a way that I felt that all previous interpretations I had heard were by comparison tame and uninspired [1]. She explained that there were four characters in the song, starting with the narrator, who should be almost 'matter of fact'. Then the father should be warm and comforting at the beginning but full of tragedy at the end, the son should become more and more agitated as the song progresses, but the voice of the Erlking should remain an icy whisper throughout and never become a thing of flesh and blood!

Blanche found out that I spoke fairly fluent French and this was the language she used for most of my lessons, although her English was very good when she chose to use it. Under her guidance my voice developed steadily and she introduced me to a number of songs by French composers, the majority of whom were her contemporaries. She felt, after some time, that I should make a professional début, and suggested that I should prepare two programmes – one in English to be given in France, and one in French for English audiences. She felt that these would help to launch my career. I pointed out that without including some songs of a popular nature I should have little chance of making a reasonable living and remember adding, 'But, Madame, even Maggie Teyte has had to include popular songs to appeal to a wider audience and recently sang "Smiling through" in a broadcast.' Blanche thought for a moment and then said, 'You are right, I once sang "Bird of love divine" ' and she beat her breast as she added, 'Mea maxima culpa!'

16

Further thoughts of a professional career were rudely shattered a few months later when I received my call-up papers to join the Royal Artillery in July 1940, and shortly after this Blanche, who refused to move from her home in Lancaster Gate, despite the bombing, became very ill and eventually died at the age of 79.

In 1935, following the reorganization of the educational system in East Sussex, the school at which I taught became an Infants and Junior School and all children over the age of 11 were sent to a Senior School. As a result of this I was sent to Burgess Hill Senior School and taught there from 1935 until I was called up into the army in 1940.

I was now much happier. My new headmaster had begun his career as an assistant in my father's school in Haywards Heath, and was much more sympathetic and made life much easier for me. I now had a classroom of my own and my specialist subjects were English, maths and music. Children over the age of 11 came from the surrounding villages including Ditchling, where Donald Sinden's father was the local chemist. Donald was in my class and I became friendly with his family, including his sister Joy who became a teacher and lecturer.

I think I can claim that I gave Donald his first acting part! We were studying *The Merchant of Venice* and I thought it would be a good idea to act part of it. I chose the trial scene and picked out some of the girls and boys to act out the whole of this in front of the rest of the class. Donald took the part of the Duke. He was a very quiet, well-behaved, rather shy boy and showed no signs of the talent of later years. I later took him to his first opera in London – *The Barber of Seville* – and was often invited to lunch at the weekends at the family house in Ditchling. After he left school we kept in touch and I well remember his early days when he acted as an amateur in Brighton. He was soon spotted by Charles Smith, a director of Brighton's Theatre Royal, and after some years in repertory he developed his unique talents that have brought him to the top of his profession.

Many years later I reminded him of his first acting part in *The Merchant of Venice* while he was still at school, and asked him if he had enjoyed it. His reply made us both laugh. He said, 'Not really. I

17

was much too self-conscious and the last thing I would have thought of was that I should ever want to be a professional actor!'

At the same time my record collecting had prospered in these pre-war years. I had collected many examples by Caruso, Melba, Patti, Tetrazzini and even one or two collectors' prizes including one that I looked upon as a supreme rarity. It was a fine copy of Albani's 'Angels ever bright and fair' recorded in 1904 showing the singer at the end of her career, when her voice was still a beautiful instrument, but by which time her style was, to put it mildly, very eccentric.

I was also an avid reader of *The Gramophone*, edited in those days by Compton Mackenzie and his brother-in-law Christopher Stone. They occasionally invited entries into competitions and one of these was for an essay comparing a composer and a poet. I chose Mendelssohn and Tennyson for my entry and to my delight and astonishment I was awarded the first prize. My essay was published in *The Gramophone* for June 1937 and this was was my first effort to appear in print. I was sufficiently encouraged after my successful essay to write a short article entitled 'Singing is not a science' and I submitted it for publication in *The Gramophone*. It was accepted and published in the magazine in August 1938. I had already shown it to Blanche Marchesi who gave it her blessing, and by now I was keen to continue my writing. A further opportunity arose when Sir Compton Mackenzie offered a prize for an essay on 'Why records are selling better and better'. Again I was lucky. A small panel of the editorial staff judged the entries and opinions were equally divided between two entries as to which was the better. I scraped through on the casting vote of the Editor-in-Chief! I remember my prize was an album of lieder sung by Lotte Lehmann and I treasured it for many years until the old shellac discs were transferred to a long-playing record which I bought to replace the original set. My essay appeared in *The Gramophone* for May 1939 and any further literary efforts on my part were then cut short when I joined the Royal Artillery in July 1940.

I considered myself rather unfortunate because I was 29 years and 11 months old when I was called up, and as a teacher I should have been in a reserved occupation at the age of thirty! Army life and discipline had never appealed to me and at Brighton

Grammar School I had successfully avoided joining the cadet corps. That extra month meant that I had to endure five years of frustration, since I had no opportunity to further my career as a singer, and I also missed my work as a teacher.

I remember the day I was called up I had to report to a recruiting centre in North London and from there I was taken together with a number of other 'rookies' to a camp in Watford for my initial training. I found this particularly irksome and resented the petty discipline imposed by many of the NCOs who put us through our paces. One especially obnoxious sergeant took us for rifle drill and 'entertained' us with remarks like: 'Look at my rifle – not at me. D'ye fancy me?' He was indirectly implying that we were a load of what in those days would have been called 'pansies'.

We were taken on long marches around Watford in addition to having to cope with what was called 'square bashing', and as a result of this I found that the heavy army boots soon made my feet rather badly blistered. I reported this to a medical orderly who had a rough and ready cure. He applied neat surgical spirit to my feet which resulted in a few really agonizing minutes, but which certainly did the trick and toughened up my feet considerably.

After about a month I was posted to a Heavy Artillery unit at the Royal Military Academy at Woolwich and I arrived there at the height of the London bombing. My unit, 58 HAA was a mobile one, and for some months we were moved around southeast London where we were billeted in various large private houses. My unit consisted largely of men from the east of London, and they were a cheerful, friendly lot whose everyday language was enlightened by expletives which were crude but undoubtedly expressive and which certainly added to my education! I soon realized what 'swearing like a trooper' meant, and initially this probably offended my sensitivity, but this soon wore off and my own vocabulary was considerably enriched by the frequent use of some good old Anglo-Saxon expressions which were descriptive rather than polite!

We did not stay around London for long however, and the battery eventually moved down to Exeter. I was used as a telephonist and typist and so, although our unit was an anti-aircraft one and we were actively engaged in defence against enemy planes, I saw very little of the action from the offices where I worked. From Exeter we were moved northeast across country and finally arrived near Selby in Yorkshire. We camped near a farm and I was detailed to work as a telephonist at a local farm about a mile from our camp. I spent some rather uncomfortable nights there in the large kitchen that served as an improvised office. The farmer and his wife did their best to make me as comfortable as possible and I had a palliasse filled with straw stretched out on the concrete floor for my bed. Unfortunately I had to share the kitchen with a large Alsatian dog who eyed me with obvious suspicion and growled softly but menacingly during the night whenever I changed my position! However fortunately for me he did not express his obvious disapproval in a more active manner and I survived intact after a rather unpleasant week, and was given several days' leave which I spent with my parents in Sussex. When I left the farmhouse the farmer sold me a side of 'green' bacon and gave me some of the very thick milk that a cow produces immediately after calving. My parents were delighted with the bacon which was very welcome in those days of strict rationing.

At the conclusion of my leave I was instructed to report back to the Royal Military Academy in Woolwich. My battery was being sent abroad but I was informed that I would remain in this country and work as a typist in the Royal Military Academy, and I spent the last four years of my army service there.

I recall one rather amusing occasion when I was having breakfast with Victor Peach, who was a Bank of England clerk, and who spoke with a very refined accent. Opposite us were three cockney lads and the first of these said that his wife was expecting a baby. I said, 'Well, as you're away perhaps she would be better off in a hospital'. He replied, 'Yes, perhaps you're right'. The second man said, 'Oh, I don't know, when my wife had her baby we just had a midwife'. The third man thought profoundly for a moment and then said, 'Well, what I say is f. . . the midwives'. Victor turned to me with a perfectly straight face and said in his most refined English, 'Well, this seems to me merely to complicate the situation'. And I had to keep a straight face, because I didn't want to upset the cockneys!

Life was fairly uneventful apart from occasional air-raids and I worked in the draft office for some months typing out long nominal roles of units who were being sent abroad. Finally I was transferred to the battery sergeant-major's office and was responsible for sending out daily orders. The sergeant-major, Bill Bailey, was a true gentleman and I cannot recall having heard him swear even mildly! On one occasion I was invited by the sergeant-clerk to make up a four at tennis during our recreational afternoon. I duly turned up with the sergeant who had invited me but when we arrived, our prospective opponents, two RSMs awaiting posting, refused hands down to play with a lowly lance-bombardier, as I then was. I was seething inwardly and the next morning I told Bill Bailey just what I thought of their behaviour in explicit but rather explosive language! He smiled slightly but made no comment at the time, but on the next free afternoon he invited me to play him at a game of singles. He proved to be quite a good player and certainly gave me no quarter, and eventually he won a closely-fought set 7–5! His gesture, which amounted to unspoken criticism of the other sergeant-majors, was the action of a sensitive and understanding person and one which I still recall with gratitude.

On my quarterly leaves I always came down to Sussex to stay with my parents, and on one occasion I met Donald Sinden again. He was acting locally at the very commencement of his career, and he took me to the theatre club in Brighton in premises near the Theatre Royal. It was always busy with many members of the theatrical profession there, and I visited it regularly and often met Donald when he was 'resting'.

Meanwhile my life at Woolwich proceeded fairly uneventfully, especially since, as a typist in the battery office, I was excused attendance at all parades and released from sentry duties. Nothing much happened to relieve the monotony of the daily routine apart from the usual air-raid warnings and the occasional scare when we heard the engine of an approaching flying bomb, or 'doodle bug' as we christened them. When the engine stopped we knew that this meant the imminent descent of the weapon, followed by a loud and dangerous explosion. Only one, as I recall, actually landed within the boundaries of the Royal Military Academy and there were fortunately no serious casualties on that occasion, as, although it landed in the middle of the parade ground, there was no one on parade!

Life was enlightened from time to time by visits to the Woolwich Empire where a great favourite was Nellie Wallace with her bawdy Elizabethan type of humour. I remember when she came on the stage beautifully gowned as Anne of Cleves and talked about her wedding to Henry the Eighth. She confided to the audience, 'It was a rough and ready affair – he was rough and I was ready! Ah, but you should have seen him when he came in with his cap in his hand and his feather dangling!' (Ribald laughter from the audience and a shocked look of disbelief from Nellie, who tossed her head, turned her back to the footlights and walked upstage, timing her return perfectly and adding, 'Ah, but he was every inch a bridegroom!')

There were also occasional performances at the Garrison Theatre and I remember one occasion when Tommy Trinder entertained us all immensely for an entire evening, not only with his usual act but also with his 'off the cuff' remarks which were hilarious and were the hallmark of a great comedian.

The 'doodle bugs' ceased after a while and were replaced for a short period by the even more deadly rockets, but the Germans were fighting a losing battle and with the gradual collapse of their resistance life became easier. Theatres, most of which had closed, now reopened and I began to think of my future when I should eventually be demobilized.

Before that, however, I became friendly with a family who lived in Eltham. The daughter of the house had a fine, well-trained soprano voice and we often had musical evenings at their home. On their recommendation I was engaged to sing the tenor solos in a performance of Haydn's *Creation* in Eltham. The conductor of the orchestra urged me to resume my musical studies and suggested that I should ask for an audition with Walter Hyde who was the principal vocal teacher at the Guildhall School of Music. He agreed to hear me and when I had obtained the necessary leave I went to Professor Hyde and took along as my solo Siegmund's 'Liebeslied' from *Die Walküre*. I had no idea that Walter Hyde had a great reputation as probably the finest

English Siegmund of his generation, nor that he had sung leading roles at Covent Garden from 1908 to 1924! If I had known I would not have dared to sing an aria for which he was famous, and would certainly have chosen something else. However, he listened carefully and agreed to take me as his pupil at the Guildhall School of Music.

Walter Hyde was not only a celebrated opera singer who had studied with Garcia, he was also an excellent teacher. He suggested that I should enter for the Tenor Scholarship at the school and prepared me carefully for the two solos set by the examiners. They were Handel's 'Where'er you walk' and Rachmaninov's 'To the children' and I was awarded the tenor scholarship and the Catherine and A. C. Howard prize. Professor Hyde congratulated me but added a word of caution saying, 'In my opinion you would be unwise to take up singing as a profession. You sing with intelligence, but your voice, although of excellent quality, has insufficient range for an operatic career.' I think I already knew this and in any case I was already 35 and felt bound to return to teaching since the education authorities had paid me my teacher's salary throughout the war. I resolved to continue singing and accepting professional engagements that suited my voice, which was more at home in concert and oratorio with its relatively limited range, seldom extending above the tenor A natural.

Meanwhile, I was able to obtain evening leave from my unit fairly easily and I regularly went to hear the Sadler's Wells Company at the New Theatre in St Martin's Lane. My great favourite was Mozart's *Cosi fan Tutte,* superbly conducted by Lawrence Collingwood and given in English by a cast which included Joan Cross, Peter Pears and Owen Brannigan.

Another great occasion for me was a visit to the Wigmore Hall to hear Maggie Teyte, accompanied by Gerald Moore in Debussy's *Chansons de Bilitis* on 7 May 1945. This was a really emotional occasion and the great artist who knew the work so well had a sudden lapse of memory. She stopped and apologized and then explained that she had just heard of Germany's unconditional surrender and she was so overwhelmed that for the moment she had found it difficult to concentrate under such wonderful and exceptional circumstances. However she soon started again and after this was at her very best for the rest of the evening.

After the concert I went with a friend to the Coventry Street Corner House and we were discussing the concert when a gentleman who was sitting at the next table leant across and asked us if we had enjoyed the performance. I said that we had loved every minute of it and he said that he too had found it a most moving experience. He then introduced himself. He was the wonderful accompanist Ivor Newton who was having a night off and was in the audience!

A few months later, thanks to a friend of mine who had recently been demobbed and who had queued for tickets, I was able to go to the reopening of the Sadler's Wells Theatre on 7 June 1945 for the world première of Benjamin Britten's great opera *Peter Grimes*. Reginald Goodall was the excellent conductor and a strong cast including Peter Pears, Joan Cross, Edith Coates and Owen Brannigan gave a superb performance which was overwhelming in its dramatic intensity. I had not read the poem by George Crabbe on which the opera is based, and so the tragic story had an even greater impact for me. I left the theatre emotionally drained.

With the defeat of the Germans and the ending of the war in Europe things became much more relaxed and evening leave was readily available. I took the opportunity of going to the theatres in London as often as funds would allow. One memorable evening I saw the fine American actors Lynn Fontanne and Alfred Lunt in Noel Coward's delightful comedy *Private Lives*. They gave virtuoso performances and I enjoyed it so much that I paid two more visits to the show. '

Life now proceeded fairly smoothly and I was already thinking of the day when I should be demobbed and be able to resume my life as a teacher, with music very much on my mind as well. Eventually the happy day arrived, and on 25 September 1945 I was given my balance of pay and presented with an appallingly ill-fitting suit plus the necessary etceteras!

I left the Royal Military Academy having been pressed into various valedictory libations by my friends, and the celebrations

24

were to continue at Woolwich station and at East Croydon where I said a final bibulous farewell to the sergeant-clerk with whom I had worked for nearly four years. By this time I was more than a little inebriated and I arrived at Haywards Heath station in a sort of drunken haze. I reached home eventually in a state which dismayed my parents who were convinced that army life had turned me into an alcoholic! However the next few days made them realize that I had really changed very little from the sober teacher of my pre-war existence, and after a short period of leave I rejoined my school at Burgess Hill.

[1] Blanche had one great handicap as far as a singing career was concerned. Her voice was not really large enough for the dramatic talent which she possessed, and its quality was rather indifferent. She had been expertly trained by her mother and had an almost perfect technique, and her powers of interpretation were quite superb. She always said that Melba did her best to ruin her career but this was certainly untrue, for the Australian soprano whose voice Mathilde Marchesi described as a 'silvery wonder' had nothing to fear by comparison. Melba spoke rather patronizingly about 'poor Blanche' and Blanche, who despised Melba's lack of any real histrionic ability, was scathing in her criticisms of Melba's rather restricted repertoire.

Blanche made some recordings in Berlin in 1906 for the German branch of the Gramophone and Typewriter Company and she told me that the studio was comparatively small but they managed to squeeze in an orchestra of sorts. The leader was so close to her that she was expecting his bow to poke into her eye at any moment. The atmosphere was stifling and the recordings were rushed through all in one session.

The discs were never issued in England and Blanche insisted that this was due to the machinations of Melba, but this seems quite unfounded. The discs were indifferently recorded even by the standards of 1906, and the titles which Blanche chose were not likely to have a wide popular appeal. One or two of them, however, are superb examples of great singing. The final phrase of 'Im Mai' is, as Blanche herself boasted, 'Un véritable tour de force' while her coloratura in 'L'Été' is superb. Her trills in this and in 'Bist Du bei mir' are wonderfully closely-knit and attacked fearlessly without any preparation. The voice, as recorded, sounds lacking in resonance and vibrance and this would certainly have limited the appeal of the records. She made some tests for Columbia shortly after this but these were never issued. If they had been in any way a rival to Melba's 'G & T' records, Columbia would obviously have been only too keen to release them.

After this Blanche made no further commercial recordings but at about the same time as her sensational recital at the Wigmore Hall in 1938 at the age of 75 she made some private recordings which she sold herself from her home in Lancaster Gate, and these were also issued in America by the International Record Collectors' Club.

3

From Tenor to Teacher

Now that army life was finally behind me I spent about three weeks becoming gradually acclimatized to the unusual freedom of life in 'civvy street'. I eventually received a letter from the Chief Education Officer for East Sussex telling me to report to the school in Burgess Hill where I had taught before the war, and I soon settled back into my life as a teacher. As before, my subjects were English, maths and music, and it was also hoped that I would write and produce a school pantomime for Christmas.

When I first met the form for which I had special responsibility I thought it would be a good idea to break the ice by asking the children to tell me their surnames as I pointed to them. Everything went quite smoothly to begin with until one boy called out his name: 'Ball, sir!' This caused one or two hastily repressed sniggers from the rest of the class who were also anxious to see what my reaction might be. I managed to retain my composure and quickly passed on to the next boy as nonchalantly as possible. I later realized that the boy was not deliberately trying to embarrass me. His name was David Ball, and after all, what else could he possibly have said? However I'm quite sure that he relished the opportunity of addressing a teacher in that way!

Shortly after I arrived at the school the deputy head who had been in a reserved occupation because he was in his middle forties, was taken ill and most tragically a week later he died to the general regret of teachers and children, because he was a most likeable and popular figure. There was still a great shortage of male teachers and no doubt for this reason I was promoted to the post of deputy head despite my lack of experience. My headmaster, Mr Barnden, was most helpful and I soon settled down to my new responsibilities which brought with them a welcome increase in salary.

Shortly after this a young man who had been an officer in the Royal Navy during the war arrived at the school. His name was Peter Court and I soon found out that he was a really excellent pianist. The headmaster asked me to be responsible for music throughout the school and it was soon arranged that I should be assisted by Peter. We doubled up classes for singing lessons, and often had the ridiculously large number of 60 or more children to cope with. However we managed quite well by teaching them well-known light classical and folk songs with me leading the singing and Peter presiding at the piano.

About the same time, within a month of my returning home, I had a telephone call from the secretary of a local operatic society in East Grinstead, a small town about 12 miles north of my home in Haywards Heath. They were putting on *The Pirates of Penzance* in two weeks' time and at the last moment their tenor had had to withdraw. They had been given my name by the secretary of another society and asked if I could help. I immediately agreed, and did not mention that I had never played the part before and indeed had never even seen this particular opera. The society agreed to pay my travelling expenses plus a small fee. I worked hard in the evenings and at rehearsals, and by the time of the dress rehearsal I was word and note perfect. It was an exciting challenge for me and I loved it. Within two months of being demobbed I was doing my first show!

Almost immediately after this I was approached by a man whom I had met in my pre-war days with the Lindfield Operatic Society. He had moved to Brighton, where he had a printing business and a stationery shop and he had formed the South Coast Light Opera Company. They were putting on *The Mikado* at the Theatre Royal and I was offered the leading tenor part of Nanki Poo, which I already knew. I jumped at the opportunity.

The founders of the society were Bernard Pullinger and Frank Lord, both local businessmen and lovers of the Gilbert and

Sullivan operas. They jointly booked the Theatre Royal for a week in December 1945 and hoped that they would attract sufficient audiences to cover expenses and possibly even make a profit. They engaged Harry Drury, a well known professional producer and proprietor of a flourishing theatrical costumiers in Brighton, and they managed to raise an orchestra of local music teachers, conducted by Leonard Aldous. Harry Drury was brisk, business-like and occasionally rather cruel at rehearsals. I remember when he was dealing with the entrance of *The Mikado*, the chorus had to kneel down and bend forward so that their foreheads touched the floor. One elderly chorus gentleman had difficulty in doing this and Harry called out, 'That bald-headed old basket at the back, if he can't get down he's out!' He was equally scathing to a well-known local entertainer who was playing the role of Koko. There was some business where he had to throw a rope for me as Nanki Poo to catch and he had difficulty in throwing it anywhere near me. Finally Harry called out, 'Cut it all out, you obviously can't do what I want, just play it straight.' I was fortunately spared any of his critical remarks, for two reasons: largely because there was still a great shortage of younger men in civilian life, but also because there was an even greater shortage of tenors!

Harry Drury was however a very experienced producer and he managed to put on a very well-produced show, but he was not really a likeable man. Leonard Aldous on the other hand was a most helpful musical director and my fellow principals were all most co-operative and a delight to work with. The bass Harold Williams who played the role of the Mikado came from Lewes and later sang small roles with the Glyndebourne Company including the part of the gardener in Mozart's *Le Nozze di Figaro*. He was rather amused when he received a letter from the very famous baritone of the day (also named Harold Williams), offering him £100 if he would sing under another name so that there would be no confusion and people would not think that *the* Harold Williams was reduced to taking on small comprimario parts!

Finally, the night of the dress rehearsal arrived and I came straight from school, snatching a hasty meal at a nearby café and

28

finally reaching the theatre in good time. Donald Sinden, who was 'resting' as a very young actor, met me at Brighton station and walked down to the café near the theatre with me. For the first time I had great misgivings about appearing at the prestigious Theatre Royal before a much more sophisticated audience than I had previously encountered, and I said to Donald, 'I'm really scared. I can't think why they chose me. I can't act and I can't sing very well'. Donald gave me an old-fashioned look and said, 'It must be your dancing, John'. I relaxed and had a good laugh after that, and as far as I was concerned the dress rehearsal went very well.

Brighton and Hove had been starved of Gilbert and Sullivan during the war years and consequently we played all the week to packed houses. There was a matinée on the Thursday afternoon and the Director of Education in Lewes gave me leave of absence from the school. He was enlightened enough to realize that my theatrical experience would be of great benefit to me as a teacher, and of course he was right. Donald Sinden's sister Joy was a teacher at the school where I taught and she was in the chorus of *The Mikado* and we always travelled together to Brighton and formed a close and lasting friendship which I enjoyed until her death in 1993.

Over the next four years or so I sang in a number of Gilbert and Sullivan operas. I went to East Grinstead for *The Yeoman of the Guard*, *Iolanthe* and *The Gondoliers*, to Lewes for *The Yeomen of the Guard* and back to Brighton to the Theatre Royal for *Ruddigore*, after which the South Coast Light Opera Company ceased to function. I therefore joined the Brighton and Hove Operatic society and sang the tenor leads for them in *The Gondoliers* and finally in *The Pirates of Penzance* in the delightful little theatre on the Palace Pier. The pier of course is still there but the theatre was demolished in 1973 following a heavy storm in which it suffered severe structural damage.

Pirates was my last show in Brighton. I had just turned forty and felt that playing the tenor roles which were always juvenile leads was best left to younger people who might be less experienced but who were more able to look the part. I did however take part in performances at the Theatre Royal for the last time in 1949. I had a telephone call out of the blue asking me if I was free in the evenings of the following week. *The Heiress* was having a pre-London run in Brighton and John Gielgud had taken over as producer at the last minute. During the second act there was a scene in which the voice of a young singer who had studied in Paris was to be heard singing in a room off stage. Sir John did not like the recording which was originally used in rehearsals and which he felt was too operatic in style. Donald Sinden, who had a small part in the play, said that he knew of a tenor who knew some French songs and whom he felt might fill the bill. Peggy Ashcroft and Ralph Richardson were the stars and so, when I was invited to become the voice off-stage singing 'Plaisir d'amour' I was naturally delighted.

I arrived at the theatre on the Saturday morning prior to the week of the show and a rehearsal was in full swing. Sir John made me sing my song at various positions off-stage, until he was satisfied that I sounded like a young man singing in the next room! As I finished my song the assembled company of young men who were not on stage, including Donald Sinden, murmured polite expressions of approval and that was the end of my contribution! I actually sang outside the star dressing room occupied by Peggy Ashcroft and each night she opened her door, brought a chair forward and sat down in the entrance to her room and always thanked me when I had finished – a gesture which I much appreciated. On the other hand, Sir Ralph did not once even acknowledge my presence in the theatre and I did not see him speak to anyone when he was off-stage. I don't think he was being in the least bit unsociable; he appeared to be completely absorbed in his role, which he played magnificently.

Although I was happy in my work at the school and in my musical activities I was saddened at home by the fact that my father was obviously not well. He developed a tremor which became steadily worse. I first noticed it when I asked him to play the accompaniment of a song I was learning, but he found it impossible to control his trembling hands and finally turned away from the piano with a quickly suppressed sob which was heart-rending. His illness was soon diagnosed as Parkinson's disease and he became progressively worse and finally died in 1949 at the age of 74. In the last week of his life he asked me to take care of my mother and I promised him that I would do so, and gladly kept my word for the rest of her long, happy life.

Meanwhile, my record collecting was gathering momentum and I spent almost all of my spare cash on old and rare records and on upgrading my equipment. I went across to Paris on several occasions, and once, when two American friends who were both record collectors accompanied me, we went to the flea market at the Porte de Clignancourt. There, I asked the owner of one of the stalls if he had any very old records of famous singers. He replied rather grudgingly in the affirmative and I asked if I could see them as I should very probably wish to buy them. He hesitated and said that he was rather disillusioned by collectors in general because he had brought them from his home on several occasions at the request of customers but they had never returned and he was naturally concerned that the same thing might happen again. I took a chance and gave him a deposit of 200 francs and asked him to bring the records in the afternoon. He was as good as his word and my friends could scarcely believe what they were seeing. It was a superb collection, a veritable Aladdin's cave of treasures! There were about 50 of the early red label celebrity records, all of the period 1902 to 1904, and manufactured by the Gramophone and Typewriter Company. They were in mint condition too, and many of them were in their original envelopes. We were able to buy them all at a very reasonable price and there were examples by Calvé, Caruso, Plançon, Battistini, Maurel and the greatest treasure of all for me – a copy of the 'Berceuse' from *Harold*, sung by the legendary soprano Félia Litvinne accompanied on the piano by the great pianist Alfred Cortot. My friends and I divided the records as fairly as we could and I returned home with my share which greatly increased my number of major rarities. I had always been an ardent admirer of the art and voice of Caruso and I began to wonder if it might be possible to acquire a complete collection of the great singer's recordings, although it seemed an almost impossible task for there were over 200 of them and some were very rare indeed. However it was a sort of pipe dream which occupied my thoughts and in the meantime I gradually added to my number of the great

31

Neapolitan's discs and just hoped!

In early 1949 a firm of record dealers in Brighton (Ross Court and Co.), who knew of my interest and had seen my occasional articles in *The Gramophone*, had invited me to edit a small magazine which was to deal exclusively with the historical side of record collecting. I agreed and *The Record News* appeared for the first time in July 1949. I was fortunate in enlisting the help of many internationally famous collectors including P G Hurst, Eric Bernard, Hugh Harvey, Paul Wilhelm of Germany, Roberto Bauer of Italy and Naomi Jacob. They all willingly gave their services and thanks to their generosity the little magazine was successfully launched. I knew that Bernard Shaw had been a music critic in his early days and that he had heard many of the great singers of the past and so, with the approval of Ross Court and Co., I wrote to him asking if he might be willing to contribute an article discussing the decline in the technique of singing since the so-called 'golden age of opera'. I pointed out that we were a small magazine and could only offer £20 (the equivalent of about £200 today), but that an article by him would greatly add to our prestige. I had no reply, but then several months later I happened to buy a copy of a weekly called *Answers*. To my annoyance and disgust I found in it an article by Bernard Shaw saying that in his opinion the standard of singing had vastly improved in recent years and that many of the famous singers of the 1880s and 1890s lost their voices after a few years and that he considered Heddle Nash the superior of most of the tenors he had heard in his youth. Of course he did not mention singers like Patti, Melba, Lilli Lehmann or Edward Lloyd and a host of others who retained many of their powers into their sixties or even seventies. I was annoyed because he had obviously made use of my suggestion, without any acknowledgement, to write more or less the opposite of what I had suggested, and I felt that he was being deliberately provocative. It did not lessen my admiration for him as a great playwright but it certainly did not increase my appreciation of him as a person!

The *Record News* lasted for 20 months and then Ross Court and Co. decided to move to Canada. After a short while they revived the magazine and I continued to edit it for a short time, but I found it too difficult and not really practicable in view of their being so far away, and so I reluctantly decided to stop my work for them as editor, although I continued to write the occasional article.

Almost immediately after this I was invited by Tony Pollard, who was the editor of *The Gramophone* to revive the feature 'Collectors' Corner' and I was happy to do so for the next few years. Then I was contacted by the editor of the *Record Review* (later to become *Hi-Fi News and Record Review*) and asked to contribute a series entitled 'Historically Speaking' on much more favourable terms, and for a number of years I wrote for the magazine continuing as a reviewer of vocal and operatic records until the late 1980s.

Now that I had decided to stop singing the tenor roles in the Gilbert and Sullivan operas and was writing regular articles, I thought I would like to try my hand as a singing teacher. I had after all studied with two eminent teachers, Blanche Marchesi and Walter Hyde, and I felt that I might be able to help young singers. However, in view of my inexperience as a singing teacher I thought I would offer my services free of charge to one or two men I knew who were singing in the choruses of local operatic and choral societies. This proved a challenging and most interesting experience, and I believe that I helped quite a number of singers without however producing anyone really outstanding. Then, as I became more confident, I started teaching profession-ally. Several of my pupils took leading roles in operatic performances in Mid-Sussex and in the meantime I continued to sing in concerts and oratorios and even in the local pantomime, where I sang ballads in my role as the Demon King! On one occasion my brother's two little daughters, aged 7 and 5 respectively, were staying with me and I went up every night to give them a bedtime kiss. Then they saw the pantomime, and I can only assume that I was very convincing in my role for, after the performance, when I went up to their room I was greeted with shrieks of horror and it was only after the hasty arrival of my brother that they could be comforted and settled down to sleep.

In 1952 we had a general inspection of the school and one of the education advisers from Lewes told me that he had had good reports of my work and suggested that I should apply for the headship of a local primary school. I was not terribly ambitious but I was then in my early forties and my headmaster, with whom I found it easy to work, was approaching retirement. I wondered how I should get on with a new and much younger principal and I decided to take the plunge and apply for the headship of Junction Road County Primary School in Burgess Hill. A few weeks later I was given an interview by the school managers and a representative from the Education Office in Lewes. There were four other candidates who were considered at the same time and to my surprise I was offered the post of headmaster from the beginning of the autumn term in September 1953.

4

Changing Times

The year 1953 was a very important one in my life, when I started as headmaster of Junction Road County Primary School with departments for infants from the age of 5 to 7, and for juniors from 7 to 11. I had spent all my teaching life (with a break of five years when I was in the army) in Burgess Hill, and now I was returning to the school where I had started as a young assistant in a very different capacity. I already knew a number of teachers there and I was a little apprehensive as to what to expect when I returned in very different circumstances. My predecessor was a strict disciplinarian of the old type and I soon realized that I should have to make some changes in the general running of the school. The children had been made to line up in the playground when school commenced and then they marched into morning assembly stamping their feet with a vigorous 'Left! Right!' precision. I found this embarrassing although of course I expected the children to come to assembly in an orderly manner. It was just the typically Victorian approach that worried me and which I was able to relax gradually.

I also made it clear to my staff that I disapproved strongly of corporal punishment. I placed great emphasis on good relations with the parents and started a Parent-Teacher Association with a committee consisting equally of parents and teachers, with me as the chairman. I felt that if there was a good and friendly relationship between teachers and parents the children would feel more secure, whereas if there was parental opposition the children would naturally side with their parents and be less happy at school. I believe I made the school a much happier place and

35

certainly there was little bad behaviour on the part of the children. The staff too soon appreciated the change and were 100% behind me.

My secretary for the first two years was an ex-army sergeant-major who greeted me every morning with a 'Good morning Sir!' as he clicked his heels. He took great pride in supervising the running of the school canteen, which certainly provided excellent meals. On the other hand he could not type and was completely hopeless on the secretarial side of his work. He was also, in a way, a male version of Mrs Malaprop. He always referred to 'foolscrap paper' and I must say I was rather relieved when he decided to retire and I was able to find a marvellous lady secretary who had had considerable business experience.

At that time Burgess Hill was growing rapidly and it was necessary over the next few years to build some prefabricated classrooms to accommodate the increasing number of pupils, and eventually to erect an entirely new infant block and a large and splendid assembly hall.

That year was a very busy year for me in other ways too. I had sung solos professionally with the Burgess Hill Choral Society, whose founder and director was George Linehan, and I suggested to him that we might consider starting a local operatic society with George as musical director and myself as producer. We managed to interest a number of people who were keen to form a chorus and we invited others who were well known as local singers to undertake the principal roles. Our first show was *The Pirates of Penzance* and the leading tenor was a pupil of mine. We were able to hire a hall belonging to St Andrew's Church in Junction Road and put on a successful show, which encouraged us to continue, and we produced Gilbert and Sullivan operas there for a number of years until the building was unfortunately burnt down and we transferred our activities for a few years to a hall in Oakmeads Secondary School.

The second show we did was *HMS Pinafore* which I was to produce in addition to taking the part of the Captain. My tenor pupil was playing Ralph Rackstraw and it was obvious on the opening night that he was very far from well and early the next morning he rang up to say that he was suffering from influenza and had a very high temperature and would not be able to come. Unfortunately, as we were a small society we had no understudies and there was nothing for it but to make a major switch-round. I took over the tenor part of Ralph Rackstraw which I had previously taken 18 years before, the person playing Dick Deadeye became the new captain and a member of the chorus stepped in as Dick. I arranged for the principals concerned to come to my school and we rehearsed in my office for the entire day, leaving the running of the school to my deputy. The performance that evening went surprisingly well, without the voice of the prompter being heard, but it was not an experience I would have cared to repeat.

A year or so later I met a lady who was affectionately known by her many friends in Burgess Hill as 'Bee Brown'. She had been a member of the D'Oyly Carte Opera Company under her maiden name of Beatrice Elburn and had sung many leading mezzo-soprano roles with them until her early retirement upon her marriage to a naval Captain. 'Bee' was a delightful, warm-hearted person and her voice was still excellent, so I persuaded her to join our society and also to help me as joint producer. We were putting on *The Yeoman of the Guard* and she played the role of Dame Carruthers with an easy elegance, which was an inspiration to us all. I shall never forget the way she spoke the lines: 'Silence, you silly girl, you know not what you say. I was born in the old keep and, please God, I shall die and be buried in it, and there's not a stone in its walls which is not as dear to me as my own right hand'. She said these lines with a quiet conviction, which was deeply moving. 'Bee' not only played the part superbly but her help and advice as co-producer were invaluable.

After this I was so busy with school affairs, teaching, singing, and writing articles for *The Gramophone* and subsequently for *Hi-Fi News and Record Review* that I was happy to hand over future productions to a lady who carried on in the same tradition, and as a result, 40 years or so later, the society is still thriving.

There is another reason for my remembering 1953, for it was then that a group of opera enthusiasts and record collectors decided to form a society which was to meet monthly to play records of famous singers of the past. It was to be called 'The

Recorded Vocal Art Society' and no doubt because I was reasonably well-known among collectors through my writings, I was invited to become the first president – an honour which I gladly accepted. During those early years we were fortunate in persuading a number of personalities well-known in the musical world to address our meetings, including singers of international reputation like Lady Harty (Agnes Nicholls) and Dame Eva Turner, while Lord Harewood and P. G. Hurst also enlivened our evenings with their interesting talks.

My record collecting prospered during the 1950s. I had completed my set of the 1902 discs of Emma Calvé and of the 'Warsaw Battistinis' and had even managed to acquire excellent copies of the four titles which Emma Albani recorded in 1904. Even more exciting was the prospect of completing my Caruso collection. I had managed to find good examples of all the HMV and Victor issues and somehow had even added five of the fabulously rare Blue Zonophones. I still needed two. One was 'La Donna è mobile', and on a visit to Paris I paid my usual pilgrimage to the 'Boite à disques' in the Rue du Louvre and asked the owner if he had any special rarities which I might like. To my amazement he produced a mint copy of the very rare Zonophone I was looking for and I spent my spare cash on this and returned home in triumph. Still one title eluded me – 'Luna fedel', and I realized that my chances of ever finding this were very remote indeed. Then I noticed that there was a programme on one of the commercial television stations hosted by Anthony Wedgwood Benn (before he was involved in politics) and viewers were invited to write in and describe any items of a collectable nature that they particularly wanted. I wrote in and mentioned my particular 'want' and was delighted when I was invited to appear on the programme, bringing with me a tape of my favourite Caruso disc. Anthony Wedgwood Benn was a charming host and soon put me at my ease, and my request for a copy of 'Luna fedel' was duly broadcast. There were, however, no replies and I had almost given up hope when I was having lunch in London with a collector friend, Gordon Whelan, the son of the music-hall star, Albert Whelan, and I found he had a copy of the record I wanted. I offered him £50 for it (this was a very fair price in those days) and he said he would think it over. Eventually after a good deal of persuasion on my part he agreed to let my buy the disc and I went home delighted, having at last completed my collection of all Caruso's published recordings.

Shortly after this the first long playing records were released and the possibility of dubbing the 78 r.p.m. discs onto the new medium soon began to interest dealers and collectors. Eventually the late Ronald Phillips of 'Collectors' Corner', Monmouth Street, invited me to transfer all my Caruso records onto open reel tape and in a few months the first virtually complete collection of Caruso's recordings appeared on the Olympus label. There have since been several reissues of all the great tenor's recorded output, greatly improved in sound quality. The one that I have complete on CD is the Pearl set with 'technical preparation' by Ward Marston. However I can at least claim that I was the first in this particular field.

The only other collector whom I knew and who had every Caruso record was Canon Drummond of Leicester. I had known him for some years and was able to find a record for him which he needed to complete his collection. It was the 'Dai campi' from Boito's *Mefistofele* recorded in Milan in March 1902 and replaced in November of that year when the matrix of the original issue was damaged. We met in London and I handed to him the precious record he required. We kept in touch for many years afterwards until his death at the age of 100. Around 1960 he suggested that we should write a book giving particulars of all Caruso's records. He was to supply details of recording dates and of their release and withdrawal from circulation and I was to provide the musical criticisms of all the discs. I was also to undertake the necessary typing and this proved quite a problem, as Canon Drummond was already in his eighties and his writing was often extremely difficult to decipher! However, eventually the typing was finished and we found a publisher, Sidgwick & Jackson. Canon Drummond wrote to Sir Compton Mackenzie and asked if he would write a foreword and he kindly consented to do so, and most generously refused to take a fee. The little book entitled *The Recorded Legacy of Enrico Caruso* was finally published in 1960 in a limited edition of 1,000 copies and was soon sold out. Since its publication further research has revealed that some of the suggested dates for the Pathé and Zonophone recordings were incorrect but on the whole there has been little to change apart from the fact that Caruso almost certainly transposed a few arias including 'Che gelida manina' and sang them a semitone lower than in the published scores.

A highlight of 1955 for me was a visit to Pinewood film studios. Donald Sinden rang me up and asked me if I would like to go with him for a day during the Easter holidays to see something of the famous studios where he was making a film called *An Alligator Named Daisy*. He suggested that as the filming started at about 7 am that I should stay overnight in his house in Hampstead and after a very early and hasty breakfast he took me by car to Pinewood.

When we arrived, filming was already in progress and I was given a seat to watch what was going on. The film was a rather silly one but the host of stars who took part was quite staggering. I can't remember all of those who were involved, but among those I met were Diana Dors, Roland Culver, Frankie Howerd and James Robertson Justice. Diana Dors and Roland Culver were waiting to do their turn and in the meantime they were filling in the time by exercising their brains with the *Daily Telegraph* crossword. Diana, who was a very unassuming and charming person, invited me to join them and I managed to help them with one or two clues. They were shooting a scene which involved a maid going along lengthy corridors in a large house, and they used the same set over and over again, changing various pieces of furniture and pictures so that in the finished version it appeared that the lady concerned was walking along vast stretches of hallway. After lunch, at which I met Frankie Howerd who had brought his boxer dog with him, Norman Wisdom who was making a different film, Kay Kendall, and Stanley Holloway, we watched a scene from another film where Norman Wisdom was supposed to swing across a room clutching a candelabra as he swayed precariously from side to side. He had a stand-in for the most difficult stunts and it was most interesting to see how the whole dangerous business was undertaken.

I was also able to visit the make-up room where there were a few wigs, which were used by a well-known actor who was almost bald! The day finished much too quickly for me and I realized how much hard work had to go into what was, in the finished film, quite a short interlude.

During this period I paid my first of many visits to Italy in company with my mother and we stayed in Stresa on the Lago di Maggiore. I had previously written to Roberto Bauer who was the leading Italian collector of early operatic recordings and whose book *The New Catalogue of Historical Recordings* is still the major work in this particular field. Roberto was a wealthy Italian connoisseur and was also the talent scout for the Metropolitan Opera, New York. He invited me to have lunch with him and I noticed that when he played a record he bent forward and almost touched the turntable with his face and he often dropped the pick-up very carelessly upon some of his priceless records but they apparently survived without damage! He shared his elegant apartment with his cousin, Otto Muller, who taught singing in Milan, and when I visited him the room was filled with students whose conversation was almost entirely devoted to the latest operatic news. Roberto spoke very good English and invited me to lunch saying 'In your honour we have roast beef!' It was delicious but really I would have preferred a typically Italian meal!

The following year I went, again with my mother, to Venice during the summer holidays and like most people I fell so completely under the spell of that beautiful city that I was determined to return there at the earliest possible opportunity. While I was there I was able to visit a museum which belonged to an Italian gentleman who had collected an astonishing number of early phonographs and gramophones as well as a sprinkling of early records. The collection was housed in a disused church, but when I returned to Venice a year or so later I was unable to find out what had happened, for the museum had obviously been disbanded and no trace was left.

In 1960 I received a letter from a Belgian dealer in Brussels who had been given my name by an English collector. He offered me a collection of early recordings including six blue Zonophones and ten red G&Ts, all apparently in excellent condition, but the most precious of all was an Odeon of 1904 sung by the great French baritone Jean Lassalle. I made what I felt was a very fair offer and this was accepted and I went to Brussels the following weekend and returned with my treasures which were soon added to my collection.

On a later occasion I went with two friends, Vivian Liff and George Stuart, to Maastricht in Holland to buy a large quantity of early records belonging to the well-known Dutch authority Leo Riemens who will always be remembered for his work on the biographical dictionary of singers entitled *Grosses Sanger-lexicon*. We stayed at an hotel just across the border in the Belgian town of Liège and visited Leo in the evening to discuss arrangements over dinner for the purchase of the records. It was decided that we should return the next morning, hoping to complete the deal. We duly arrived and were shown upstairs where the records were stored on shelves, and we bought the entire collection, sharing it out as to our particular interests. While we were examining the records, Leo's little 6-year-old daughter, who was a fiend incarnate, decided to inflict her particular brand of sadism on Vivian by repeatedly kicking him on the shins! It is surprising what powerful kicks a monster of 6 can deliver and Leo did absolutely nothing to restrain the little horror! However, eventually we left together with all the records and now in retrospect we can afford to laugh at what was, at the time, anything but amusing!

By the early 1960s I was taking my teaching of singing much more seriously and I felt it would be of inestimable value to me as a teacher if I could study the music of the French school with Maggie Teyte, who I understood was teaching in London. She was a pupil of the great Jean de Reszke and was greatly admired by Debussy who praised her Mélisande. I wrote to her and asked for an audition and I had a reply in her typically terse manner. She said that she could see me if I came to the Wigmore Street studios where she was teaching. She added 'the damage will be £5'. I duly arrived on a Saturday morning in 1963 and Dame Maggie opened the door and motioned to me to sit down, as she was giving a lesson to a young Canadian baritone. She was smaller than I expected, having only seen her previously on the concert platform, and she was the very antithesis of a flamboyant prima donna, being dressed very simply in a grey skirt and knitted jumper, and wearing on her head a woollen beret covering her rather faded light brown hair. When the lesson was finished and her pupil had departed she asked me what music I had brought. I produced an eighteenth-century French chansonette arranged by Weckerlin and entitled 'Jeunes fillettes'. She seemed to like my singing of it and agreed to give me lessons, adding, 'You're not a young man, how do you think I could help you?' I replied that I had studied with Blanche Marchesi and Walter Hyde and was now teaching myself, and I felt that her experiences as a pupil of Jean de Reske and Debussy would help me greatly in my understanding and appreciation of French song. She replied, 'OK, we'll see what we can do'. She then gave me some exercises which she said would help me to float the voice lightly on the breath and told me to practise these before I returned. She also suggested that I should bring along my copy of the Duparc songs, which I mentioned I had been studying.

When I arrived for my first lesson, after giving me some fairly simple exercises which she said would help me to 'place' my voice, we started looking at Duparc's 'Chanson triste'. Maggie commented after I had sung it, 'It doesn't sound quite right for your voice – let's do it again'. I repeated it and she said, 'It still doesn't sound quite right – can you suggest why?' I replied that when I was younger I had always sung it a third higher and Maggie remarked, 'Why have you changed?' I explained that I was now 53 and found it easier. She said: 'That is the answer of a lazy man. You will sing it in the original key.' There was no arguing with her and that was that!

I enjoyed my lessons very much but was surprised at Maggie's very down-to-earth approach. On one occasion I was singing a phrase containing a triplet and she didn't like the way I was doing it. She said, 'You must make the three notes absolutely equal. Jean de Reske always called them "triolets". Do it again.' We repeated it several times, but Maggie was still not satisfied and finally banged down the lid of the piano and said, 'John, don't bugger about!' And that was the end of the lesson! I found it very difficult to reconcile her very earthy approach with the exquisitely sensitive artist who sang Berlioz's 'Absence' and so many songs of the French school, particularly Hahn, Duparc and Debussy, with such delicacy.

After the very abrupt end of that particular lesson I wondered how I should be greeted when I next arrived. I needn't have worried. She said, 'I would like you to sing at a concert given by my pupils', and when I hesitated she said, 'Why don't you want to? You've got a damn fine voice'. However I decided against it and continued my lessons for several months until she was unable to undertake so much work as she was in her late seventies and was feeling very tired.

My mother was 80-years-old in 1960, and although she was still very alert mentally and showed little sign of her age in her general appearance, she was becoming less mobile and the doctor treated her for osteoarthritis. She had gone with me on my summer holidays every year to various countries including Italy, France, Switzerland, Germany and Austria, but it was now becoming more difficult for her to travel. She decided in 1963 to visit the Orkney Islands as a last fling, and so we booked a coach tour, which started from London. After overnight stops at York and Aberdeen we eventually reached the small port of Stromness where we stayed for a week, going on excursions to places of interest including Kirkwall, the capital. After a rest on our first day we decided to go for a walk along the main street of Stromness when to our amazement a woman came up to me and said, 'Are you Mr Freestone from Burgess Hill?' She then explained that she was born in Stromness but had worked for some time in London where she had met her future husband. He was a bank clerk and shortly after their marriage he was transferred to Burgess Hill. While she was there she had heard me sing in a few concerts. Then, upon the death of her husband, she had decided to return to her native town to spend the rest of her days there. Quite a simple explanation, but what an amazing coincidence!

After that trip my mother was happy to remain at home and I made sure to take her for a car ride every evening except in the middle of winter when it was too dark and cold. I felt that it was necessary for me to take short holidays on my own and always arranged for a lady friend to stay with her while I was away. My favourite breaks were in Paris and Brussels where I loved to visit the flea markets, looking for old records, although on one occasion I went as far as Lyon in central France to buy an important collection. As my mother's arthritis became more severe I gradually took over the cooking (under her supervision) and this experience proved most useful. I think I can now claim to be quite a good cook!

The doctor paid my mother regular visits and eventually told me that her heart was beginning to fail, and shortly after this she had a massive coronary and did not regain consciousness.

I was heartbroken. Although I knew that she would almost inevitably die before me, when the moment of parting finally arrived I was totally unprepared for it. We had always been very close and I knew that if I was ever in any difficulty she was there to help and comfort me. Now I was totally alone.

I realized that the only thing to do was to keep myself fully occupied and so, even on the day of my mother's cremation, I went to school in the morning and left to go to the funeral service in the afternoon. There was of course much to arrange during the following week and then school closed for the Easter holidays. I made hasty arrangements for a week's break in Malta and managed to enjoy myself during the daytime when I went on a number of excursions, and I also made the acquaintance of the very well-known Maltese architect, Richard England, who made me very welcome and took me to Medina, the old capital where he was doing extensive restorations. Richard knew me because he was a record collector and had read my articles in *The Gramophone*. I also inserted advertisements in the local newspapers asking for old operatic records and I had quite a good response. It was at night, in the solitude of my room, that I was alone with my grief. Gradually however I realized that the last thing that my mother would have wished was for me to be unhappy and I gained comfort from the thought and kept myself as fully occupied as possible.

Fortunately, opportunities occurred which meant that I was very busy during the following months. I met Michael Ades who was the assistant musical adviser for East Sussex schools, and he decided to put on *Hansel and Gretel* for the newly-formed Mid-Sussex Operatic Society and asked me if I would be prepared to undertake the part of the father. It is a high baritone role and suited me very well now that I was in my sixtieth year. My stage wife was played by Marjorie Flynn who had sung principal soprano roles with the D'Oyly Carte Opera Company on tour, but had retired early upon her marriage. The two children and the witch were well cast with very good amateur singers for these characters. Rehearsals were held in a local school hall in Haywards Heath and went very well.

A young man with a very beautiful tenor voice came along to a number of rehearsals but did not take part, although he was obviously very interested. He was working on a farm near Balcombe and was waiting until a new term started at the Guildhall School of Music in London, where he was intending to study singing with Ellis Keeler. We all felt that he had a great future, and since then he has become one of the outstanding English tenors of the day. His name is Anthony Rolfe-Johnson!

Hansel and Gretel was a decided success and it was proposed that we should present *Amahl and the Night Visitors* the following year. We had two trebles, both excellent, whom Michael Ades coached and they sang the role of Amahl on alternate nights, while I took the tenor part of the old deaf king – one of the three magi. I enjoyed playing a humorous role and the whole opera went off splendidly. This was the last occasion on which I appeared in any stage work, although I continued to sing occasionally at concerts for some years.

At this time the education authority were anxious to give school-leavers the opportunity to take part in cultural weekends at further education centres at Pike House in Battle and at Stafford House in Hassocks. The idea was to help the children to make use of their leisure time in interesting and useful ways. I was approached to present an hour of music, illustrating my remarks with examples of well-loved classics recorded on tape or cassette. My first talk was to pupils from Oakmeads School, Burgess Hill. A group of about 30 young people spent the weekend at Stafford House and I was invited to the evening meal on Saturday, and gave my talk afterwards. I realized that it might be difficult to interest all these teenagers in what might loosely be called 'classical music', but I felt if I could play them various popular works in really first-class stereo sound then, that the actual quality of the reproduction would go a long way to maintaining their attention. I chose the music very carefully and explained what I was playing in some detail, as well as introducing one or two amusing anecdotes and the hour finished very successfully with some requests for encores! Some further education officers came into my talk and as a result I was recommended to other schools and for the next few years I was kept quite busy with my musical talks to school-leavers.

After the death of my mother I was of course quite free at weekends and I was eventually invited to give a musical weekend for adults taking further education at Stafford House. I invited Bryan Vickers, a friend of mine and a first-class professional pianist, to join me for the weekend devoted to the music of Mozart and this was followed later by a similar weekend dealing with the works of Schubert. I was then bold enough to telephone Dame Eva Turner whom I knew quite well by this time and ask her if she would like to come down and give a talk and possibly spend a relaxing weekend at Stafford House. She agreed and we called it 'A weekend of Opera'. Dame Eva was really marvellous and gave a most interesting talk on her great career, and altogether we had a really splendid weekend.

A number of German and Czech students spent a week at Stafford House in July 1967 and I was booked to give two talks. The young people had come to learn something of British culture and customs and my first talk was on the education system in England. This was in the morning of 14 July and the same evening I spoke about British music. I knew that there were many Czech students there and at the end of my programme I said that I would like to play a record which was a great favourite of mine. It was 'Elsa's dream' from Wagner's *Lohengrin* sung by the great Czech soprano Ema Destinnova, or Emmy Destinn as she was called in Western Europe. A young man came up to me and said how delighted he was to know that Destinn was so well known in England, and this was the beginning of a very happy friendship. The young man was Jan Kralik, now a doctor of science at Prague

47

University, and he suggested that I might like to go to Prague and meet his family. I stayed for just four days at an hotel in Prague, and when I went to pay my bill at the end of my stay I was told that Jan's father, who was a doctor of medicine, had already paid it. I was quite overwhelmed by this generosity but luckily I was able to reciprocate to some extent. Jan was in England in August 1968 when the tragic news came that Czechoslovakia had been invaded by the Russians, and he stayed with me for three days before returning to his home, having managed to telephone his parents who said it was safe for him to go back.

Then in 1969 Jan's family, consisting of his father, mother and sister, by some miracle managed to come to England for a holiday, driving all the way by car. They were unable to bring more than the merest pittance, but I was only too happy to finance them as far as I could and we managed to get a small grant from the funds of Stafford House, to give them some spending money. They were completely amazed at the shops, which were well-stocked with merchandise of all kinds, whereas in Czechoslovakia many of the stores had very little to offer.

We went to a 'prom' in London, and on another occasion we drove to Stratford-on-Avon and I booked seats for *The Merry Wives of Windsor* which I felt would be easy for my visitors to follow. We called at the theatre in the morning and I found that Donald Sinden was rehearsing there. I sent a message to him saying that I had arrived with some friends and he immediately asked the producer to spare him for a couple of hours and rehearse scenes in which he was not involved, and he showed us all over the theatre and really made a fuss of my friends who were charmed by his generosity in giving so much of his time to us.

After this I visited Czechoslovakia every year for some time and stayed with my friends in their beautiful house in Tousen, a small village some 20 miles or so from Prague. Doctor Kralik, who had been so kind and generous to me, unfortunately died shortly after this. He had been in charge of the Institute for Rheumatics and Arthritics in Prague, but he did not join the Communist Party although this would have made life easier for him. As a result his position was gradually undermined and young communist doctors were brought in to take over the active running of the institute. Dr Kralik retained his official post as principal and his salary was not reduced but he felt the loss of his authority very keenly and suffered from hypertension which eventually contributed to his early death while still in his fifties. He had been given a car for official duties, but with his death it was impossible for the family to obtain a new one and as a result it was no longer possible for me to stay with them in Tousen and I began to book in at hotels for my annual visit to Prague.

I was still teaching and so I was busy during the day during term-time but I was not happy living alone in a fairly large house. I mentioned this to our local curate. He said to me, 'Why don't you get in touch with the local grammar school and see if there are any young teachers who are looking for accommodation?' I contacted the school secretary and it happened that there were two young men who were looking for suitable rooms. They were both engaged to be married and were very happy to find decent 'digs' at what I hope was a very modest price. It worked very well as a temporary measure. At the same time I had made up my mind to retire, as I had reached the age of 60 and was already beginning to feel tired.

I carried on until the end of the summer term in 1971 when I was given a wonderful farewell by the teachers and children and later by the Parent-Teacher Association, and shortly afterwards I went on a holiday to the USA as my retirement treat! I visited Boston, Washington, New York, San Francisco and Las Vegas. I loved San Francisco and found New York very exciting but terribly hot in July. I did not like Las Vegas but it was an ideal point from which to go to the Grand Canyon by light aircraft. It was wonderful beyond words and was for me the highlight of the whole tour. I was fortunate to have as a companion one of the two young schoolmasters who had rooms in my house. He was a geography specialist and when I told him where I was going he took the opportunity to see the USA at first hand.

It was over all too soon, and when I returned I had to settle down to a new life which required considerable adjustment! Fortunately my musical experience came to the rescue and helped me to tide over the first few difficult months of my retirement.

5

Retirement: A New Life

Now that my weeks were free I was able to undertake other engagements. I was asked to give a series of lectures on opera for further education and every Friday morning for 12 weeks of the autumn term I chose one complete opera, explained the plot and gave biographical details of the composer, illustrating my talk with excerpts recorded on cassette. I took with me two loud-speakers, a cassette player and an amplifier, and was able to produce really very excellent sound with this stereo equipment, My first series of talks were very successful and I had an average attendance of over 20 people, and so I was asked to continue after Christmas with a further series of 12 lectures, and I carried this on for a number of years at the Further Education Centre in Stafford House.

I was kept quite busy with this work and at the same time I submitted my name for musical talks to the headquarters of the Women's Institute and the Townswomen's Guild. As a result of this I often gave as many as three talks a week and I was also reviewing operatic records for *Hi-Fi News and Record Review* and gave singing lessons to a number of pupils.

All this activity helped me to cope with my new situation and at the same time I decided to get a dog, as I needed companion-ship of some kind, especially during the holiday periods when my lodgers left me and went to their respective homes. I was discussing the possibility of buying a dog with a lady friend who attended my opera class and who was on the committee of the Happy Breed Dog Rescue Society. She told me that they had just received as a stray a young Labrador bitch who was in whelp, and she suggested that I might like to visit the kennels and see her. I fell in love with her immediately and took her out every day for walks in the nearby woods, but as I had arranged to go to India for a short holiday, the lady in charge of the kennels thought it would be best if I left the bitch where she was until I returned from India, after which the puppies would have been born and she would have been weaned.

In the meantime I was looking forward eagerly to my holiday in India. I had been invited by my friend Khushroo Suntook to stay with him and his family, who live in Bombay. I had met him as a result of his reading my articles in *The Gramophone*. Khushroo was, and still is, a keen record collector and he met me at Bombay airport and drove me to his large apartment where I met his wife and two children. I arrived in clothing which had been fine for an English January but which was hardly suitable for the heat of an Indian 'winter' where the temperature was in the high eighties! However, having changed into something more appropriate I was able to relax and to begin a wonderful holiday with Khushroo and his family. At that time alcohol was not readily available but my hosts knew that I liked a modest gin and tonic before my lunch and evening meal. The solution was simple. Much to the amusement of my Indian friends I was registered as an alcoholic and then the necessary drinks could be readily purchased at the local stores!

During my stay I was taken to Delhi and spent two nights at the house of the local member of parliament. From his house it was only a short car ride to visit the wonderful Taj Mahal. I had of course seen colour photographs of it but nothing could begin to convey the breathtaking beauty of this exquisite building, erected by the Mogul emperor Shah Jahan as a mausoleum for his favourite wife, Mumtaz-i-Mahal.

India is a land of contrasts. The wonderful palaces of the wealthy princes and the pitiful shacks of the poor stand almost side by side and are a reminder that for all the efforts of the various governments it will be many years before such socially unacceptable conditions are improved. Khushroo gave me a good example of one of the problems. We went out to his estate in the country, where he had a beautiful house and splendid gardens. A young man was working in the orchards there, and Khushroo told me that he was paying for the youth to go to college as he was very intelligent. However, instead of spending a second year at college after which he could have obtained decent employment, he told Khushroo that he would rather go back to his native village and live the life of a peasant with his family.

I was able to visit an excellent tailor in Bombay who made me two suits, one of a fine woollen material and the other of Indian raw silk, which I still possess and wear occasionally. However, all too soon my holiday was over and I returned to the cold of late January in England. The very next day I went to the kennels to pick up my Labrador whom I decided to call 'Mimi'. I brought her to my home and showed her a large circular basket, which I had bought for her to sleep in. The first night she duly went to her bed in the kitchen and I went up to my bedroom. Shortly afterwards I heard a little whine and I went down to try to comfort Mimi and then having stroked her and apparently settled her down I returned to my room. Again there was a whine from downstairs and this time I took her and her basket up to my room where she soon settled down and from then onwards that was where she slept. She had won the first round and continued to win most of the others for the rest of her long, and I hope happy, life.

During this time when I was living in retirement at Haywards Heath my life became more and more involved with music. I was reviewing records in *Hi-Fi News and Record Review*, giving talks professionally to various societies, and keenly collecting records of the great singers of the past. This entailed paying numerous short visits to various Italian cities, to Brussels, Vienna and Paris, and I managed to acquire a number of major rarities including several of the fabulously rare light-blue label Zonophones by Delmas, Magini Coletti, Wermez, Cucini, Torresella and Lelio Casini as well as Odeons of Lassalle and Litvinne.

At that time I could boast that I had a major collection of international importance which I had been able to purchase fairly reasonably before the prices asked by dealers increased astronomically and put them beyond my reach. One day a collector friend, Dudley Scholte, with whom I had corresponded since 1931, rang me up and told me that P. G. Hurst, who wrote

'Collectors' Corner' in *The Gramophone* for a number of years and who was rightly looked upon as the founder in England of the hobby of collecting early gramophone records, was in a nursing home at Cowfold not far from Haywards Heath. He had suffered a stroke and Dudley was bringing down by train the famous soprano Dame Eva Turner who was an old friend of P. G. Hurst. Dudley asked me to meet him and Eva at Haywards Heath station and to take them in my car to Cowfold. I was of course delighted to meet Eva socially and we made a number of journeys to visit 'P.G.' and as a result we became very good friends. I had, as I have already mentioned, heard Eva sing at Covent Garden in 1935 and also at the Dome in Brighton where she appeared as a soloist with Sir Thomas Beecham and the London Philharmonic Orchestra. However in those days she was just a distant luminary as far as I was concerned and I had no idea that I should one day come to know her so well. She told me that she had a blind sister-in-law living on the Sussex coast at Telscombe cliffs and asked me if I could meet her at Brighton station and take her by car to meet her relative. I was of course only too delighted to do so and during the course of the next few years I often took Eva by car to Florence Turner's home. Eva always insisted upon paying for the petrol on these occasions despite my protests and indeed she was always over-generous in dealing with me.

Eva told me that she had a villa in Switzerland on Lake Lugano in a village called Brusino Arsizio, and as she was seldom there herself, she let it during the summer months to holiday-makers who dealt with her agent there, the local schoolmaster. I told Eva that I would very much like to rent the villa myself for two weeks during August and in 1977 I set out with two friends, arriving in the village fairly late in the evening. Eventually, after some difficulty in locating the schoolmaster who held the keys, we reached the villa. It was, as Eva had warned me, rather shabbily furnished since she had not lived there for some years, but it was spacious and in a marvellous position on the lake-side. The accommodation consisted of a dining-room, a drawing-room and a large old-fashioned kitchen on the ground floor while upstairs there were two double bedrooms and a single one, plus a very large and rather inconvenient bathroom! On our first visit, since we arrived after dark, we could not see the wonderful view across the lake but we went out onto a flat roof above the drawing room and the sight was magical with the myriad lights of Lugano city twinkling like many coloured jewels in the distance. The next morning we were able to see the really magnificent scenery with the small but busy town of Morcote in the distance on the opposite side of the lake, surrounded by the mountains of almost alpine splendour.

We were joined in the villa by a Swiss friend who took us out in her car every day to the many tiny villages cradled on the hillsides and a special treat was a journey by funicular railway to the summit of Monte Generoso from where we could see the highest Swiss Alps, including the Jungfrau in the far distance.

In the little village of Brusino Arsizio language would have been a problem, since no one spoke English or French, had it not been for our Swiss friend. The locals spoke either Italian or German and there were many German-speaking Swiss holiday-makers who paid regular visits to Ticino.

I enjoyed the holiday so much that the following year I invited some younger friends, two of whom were schoolmasters and another, a singing pupil of mine. It was arranged that we should take my car and drive across France to Switzerland. I was a little apprehensive about driving on the continent, but my companions, who were all reliable drivers, were happy to take turns at the wheel. We stopped at Chaumont in France overnight on the way down and found a very pleasant hotel where we were able to enjoy an excellent dinner. I was so impressed that I asked the proprietor if we could book rooms for a night on the return journey. He said that this would not be possible as the hotel would be closed for two weeks for the *clôture annuelle*. I asked him if he could recommend another hotel but he said that he had a motel adjoining the hotel and that this would also be closed, but that he would leave the keys in two doors of the motel rooms and we could stay there for the night and leave the money on the beds when we left. I was very flattered by his trust and for some years after this I always stayed at his hotel on all my holidays to Brusino Arsizio.

The journey across Switzerland was a most wonderful and

My mother

My father

My parents' wedding, 1903

Myself, as Marco in
The Gondoliers, c. 1936

Myself, c. 1938

Blanche Marchesi

Walter Hyde,
Principal Vocal Teacher,
The Guildhall

At college. I am front right

Myself, centre, as Fairfax in *The Yeoman of the Guard*, c. 1955

My retirement from teaching, 1971

With my treasured portraits of Melba and Caruso

Myself and Michael, 1990

Laurence Dale, one of my pupils

Sir Donald Sinden, myself, and Eva Turner

A visit to Czechoslovakia

Myself with Phyllis, Robert and Ian

Mimi relaxing on the sofa

exciting experience. It was Whitsun and the snow was still standing in heaps on the roadside at fairly low levels. When we reached the summit of the San Gottardo pass we found that the main road was closed but eventually after much difficulty, we found a side-road, which was open, and were able to cross. After a hair-raising and somewhat precarious journey, we finally arrived in Brusino Arsizio, exhausted but very relieved.

For a number of years after this I returned regularly to Eva's villa and made sure that I had learned sufficient Italian to feel at home in the local shops and restaurants. The journey was made much easier by the opening of the San Gottardo tunnel which is a marvel of technical achievement. Dame Eva Turner's name was still remembered and she was spoken of with great affection by many people who had known her when she lived there during her operatic seasons just across the border in Italy. We often made the journey, with a brief stop at the customs, to the little town of Porto Ceresio where we enjoyed delicious meals cooked by the wife of the proprietor, at the Ristorante al Cervo. The local shopkeepers, when they found that we were staying at Eva's villa, would eagerly enquire as to her health and activities and would ask when she would return to see them all again.

I continued as usual with my talks in Sussex, and was kept very busy. I received a letter from Liverpool from a lady named Marjorie Hill, who was the secretary of the Liverpool Opera circle, inviting me to give a talk to her society, and this was apparently very successful for I continued to pay my annual visit, and for several years I gave the opening talk for the new season, commencing in September.

In the meantime I continued to visit Eva's villa every year until 1985, after which she decided to sell it. During my last stay in Brusino my friends Michael Murdon, Harry Joy and Dennis Simmons came with me and we had bought tickets for a performance of *Turandot* at La Scala Milan.

Just before we left for the villa, I had a phone call from ITV telling me that Eamonn Andrews was preparing a *This is Your Life* programme with Donald Sinden as the subject to be interviewed. I was asked if I would like to take part in the show as Joy Sinden, Donald's sister, had given them my name since I taught Donald when he was a schoolboy. I said that I would have been delighted but that I should be on holiday in Switzerland and Italy on the date concerned. I was told that would present no problem as they would fly me to London Heathrow from Milan, put me up in London for the night and fly me back to Milan the next morning! Of course I accepted gladly and spent a most interesting afternoon at a rehearsal with a 'stand in' for Donald and an even more interesting evening when the programme was recorded live. I was completely overwhelmed by the host of celebrities who appeared, including Dame Anna Neagle, Sir Geoffrey and Lady Howe, Dame Judi Dench, Googie Withers, Jeffrey Archer, Patrick Cargill and many others of equal fame. It was a really delightful evening and there was a party afterwards to celebrate the occasion.

The next morning a taxi picked me up at my London hotel and whisked me off to Heathrow for the return journey. I was greeted with rather sad news. Dennis Simmons had developed serious eye trouble with a detached retina and he was determined to be treated in London. This meant that he had to leave, in company with his friend who insisted upon going with him, and as a result we had two spare tickets for *Turandot* at La Scala. I immediately telephoned Dame Eva in London and asked her if she would be interested in joining us, and to my delight and amazement she said she would love to come.

In the meantime I booked rooms for our overnight stay in Milan and met Dame Eva at the airport and accompanied her to our hotel. She was already 93 but was full of life and we arrived at La Scala in good time. I had telephoned the management of the theatre telling them that Dame Eva would be attending the evening performance, but only managed to contact a young woman who had obviously never heard of the great singer. She arrived unheralded and virtually unrecognized except by a Japanese lady who came up to us and greeted her enthusiastically! The performance went well and I still have my copy of the programme in which Eva wrote the following: 'To Jack and Michael, with lovely memories of our *Turandot* at La Scala on 18.4.85! My love and blessings and my warm thanks and appreciation of all their kindness! In very truth a red letter happening!! Always, Eva.'

It had been a rather exhausting day and as usual the performance finished fairly late. To my amazement Dame Eva was full of life and insisted upon taking us to supper at Biffi's where the staff remembered her well. I think both Michael and I were feeling very tired but Eva was the life and soul of the party and was still as fresh as a daisy until we finally returned to the hotel.

Eva was always a charming companion and her knowledge of operatic music was encyclopaedic. On the other hand she was remarkably naïve in general conversation.

I remember her secretary and companion, Anne Ridyard, telling me that on one occasion when Eva was entertaining some friends, the opera *Hansel and Gretel* by Humperdinck was being discussed and one of the party said, 'The role of the Sandman is always sung by a lady. It's a transvestite part, isn't it?' Eva replied 'No dear – a mezzo-soprano one'. Eva was by then in her nineties and would not have understood 'transvestite'.

Upon another occasion Anne Ridyard who was an outspoken member of the party said, 'There are two things I like stiff and one is redcurrant jelly'. In her delightful innocence Eva said, 'And what is the other, dear?' and was completely nonplussed by the general hilarity her question had aroused!

6

Brighton

I have let my enthusiasm for my friendship with Eva Turner and my wonderful holidays at her villa run away with me, but now I must return to my life after I retired. I mentioned that after the death of my mother I continued to live at my house in Haywards Heath and let rooms to young schoolmasters. This continued until 1974 when I had a telephone call from my cousin Evangeline Webber, or Ena as we called her. She lived in Brighton in a delightful bungalow in the Patcham area. Her husband had died a few years earlier and she now shared the bungalow with the family's old housekeeper who was also a widow. She phoned to tell me that another bungalow in the same road had recently been put on the market and wondered whether I would be interested in buying it. I had always loved Brighton and many of my musical activities had been centred there and so I drove down from Haywards Heath the same day and telephoned the local house agent who was selling the property, asking him to meet me there. I fell in love with it immediately and arranged straightaway to pay a deposit on it while I sold my house in Haywards Heath.

The bungalow consisted of a really large living room with French windows opening out onto a splendid garden, a separate dining room, two bedrooms and a large old fashioned kitchen and the usual offices. Across the road, facing the front of the bungalow was a small copse and beyond that was a large space of grassland with ornamental shrubs, while at the bottom was a lily pond surrounded by numerous flower beds.

I was fortunate in selling my house at Haywards Heath quite quickly and soon moved into my bungalow in Woodland Way,

Patcham – a residential area of Brighton built on downland and only a mile or so from the centre of the town. One member of the household who obviously approved was Mimi, who loved walking through the copse on the other side of the road!

I was very happy to be near my cousin Ena for we had always been great friends and she was my only close relative, apart from my brother who lived in Wiltshire and my two nieces who had both already married and left my brother's home.

It was a great relief to be able to relax in Ena's company and she introduced me to a number of her friends, including the playwright Philip King who lived only two doors from me.

Other friends were Margaret and Ben Tapner who lived in Burgess Hill and Ben was an architect who had designed the necessary plans for an extension to Ena's bungalow. Before long I had arranged with Ben to help me in a similar way. I had an additional bedroom and bathroom built in the roof and then approached Sussex University and told them that I would be prepared to let a 'bed-sit' to a suitable student, and for the next five years I was fortunate in finding excellent tenants who were quiet and were apparently only too happy to find decent accommodation at what I was assured was a very reasonable price.

Having settled into my new home, I soon found plenty to do. I continued giving talks on music to various groups. I made regular visits to Haywards Heath, where blind people met at a large private house and were entertained by visiting speakers. I also went to a similar group at Peacehaven, entertained a large club for arthritics in Hove Town Hall and in Lancing, and also spoke to a number of Women's Institutes and Townswomen's Guilds in various parts of Sussex. I also started my annual visits to Liverpool to talk to the Opera Circle and to Bournemouth for my recitals for the Bournemouth Gramophone Society. I also went on with my series of operatic lectures at Stafford House and had a growing number of singing pupils whom I taught in the evenings.

Dr John Gardiner, the music master of Brighton and Hove Grammar School rang me up in late 1974. He had a pupil who was to sing the role of Ralph in the Christmas production at the school of *HMS Pinafore* and he felt that the young man would benefit from a few singing lessons. I arranged for him to come for an audition. He was 17 and I gave him a few simple exercises to sing. There was something very striking about the voice although he had very little idea of how to use it. The timbre was already very beautiful and decidedly that of a tenor, although at this early stage he found high notes above G very difficult. There are several top As in 'Pinafore' for Ralph to sing, and after a few lessons and sets of exercises he managed to sing the top notes reasonably well. He was a good musician and a very intelligent young man and was also very keen to improve his singing, so that within a year I felt that he had something quite exceptional. Together we worked at some arias and songs and I entered him in the Brighton and Worthing Competitive Music Festivals singing 'Una furtiva lagrima' from Donizetti's *L'Elisir d'amore*. He sang very beautifully and won first prize in both tenor classes.

I had always been very unwilling to suggest to any of my singing pupils that they were sufficiently gifted to consider a professional career, but here was obviously an exception. Fortunately, during this period I invited Eva Turner and her companion Ann Ridyard to come down to a small luncheon party and they were driven down by Brian Griffiths, who was an excellent pianist and played for some of Eva's pupils. My tenor was also a member of the party and before lunch I asked Eva if she would hear him and give me her opinion of his talent. She consented, with the proviso that only myself and Brian should be present in the room where my pupil sang. She listened most attentively and after he had sung 'Una furtiva lagrima' she said, 'You are not sustaining the tone on the breath to the end of certain phrases, but I consider that you have a great deal to offer.' That was sufficient for me, and I then talked to the young man's parents and suggested that he might consider a musical career, which he very much wanted. They eventually agreed and it was proposed that he should try for a choral scholarship to Oxford. Personally I was against this as I felt that he would be trained in the English cathedral-school tradition, whereas I wanted him to sing in a more operatic style for which his voice was eminently suited. It was then decided that he should go to the Guildhall School of Music where I had myself studied, and he quickly made tremendous progress. He studied there for three or four years, mainly with Rudolph Pierne, and shortly after he left the Guildhall he was engaged to sing the leading tenor role in Rossini's *Cenerentola* at Glyndebourne – a tremendous honour for a young and relatively inexperienced artist. He has since sung leading roles at Covent Garden, the London Coliseum, in Salzburg, Paris and Vienna, and is now firmly established among the younger tenors of the day. His name is Laurence Dale.

I spent Christmas 1974 in Italy near Rome, as the guest of Betty and Keith Hardwick. Keith was still in the Navy with the rank of Commander, and he was attached to NATO, where his excellent Italian was much appreciated in his work as an interpreter. He was allotted a lovely villa in a small village near Rome, called Anguillara Sabazia, on the shores of a small lake. Since I was there for the Christmas holidays Keith was able to spend his leave taking me into Rome for a delightful dinner in a restaurant in the *Trastevere* area, and we also visited the *Teatro dell 'Opera* for a performance of ballet and passed a memorable day in Orvieto where we had a delicious lunch and drank the local wine as an aperitif and also with the meal.

I paid my second visit to India in 1972 and Khushroo took me to some marvellous temples carved out of the solid rock and to the 'pink city' of Jaipur. We also spent a long weekend on his estate between Bombay and Poona. While in India I was given some idea of the social attitudes which still prevail among the elderly upper-class Indians. Khushroo introduced me to an old gentleman who lived in a magnificent house in Bombay surrounded by treasures of all kinds. He had a similar house in Calcutta but was actually living in very straitened circumstances. Due to depreciation, his personal fortune had largely disappeared. He did not go to his house in Calcutta any longer and could have realized a considerable sum if he had sold it together with its contents, but felt that he could not do so because it would have involved a loss of 'face' and his pride could not allow this!

My seventieth birthday was on 23 July 1980, and I decided to have a small party and buffet lunch to celebrate my having reached my 'three score years and ten'. Most of my guests were my immediate neighbours and friends including Philip King whose farces *See How they Run, Sailor Beware* and *Big Bad Mouse* earned him a small fortune, but I also invited Eva Turner and her companion Ann Ridyard, Donald Sinden and his wife Diana, and an old friend of Eva's from a different world of entertainment – Duggie Byng, famous pantomime dame and top cabaret artist of his day. Fortunately it was a beautiful sunny day and so we were able to spend most of the time talking to each other sitting on the large lawn in my garden. Eva and Donald were already a 'mutual admiration society' and the whole party went off splendidly.

Shortly after this I had a phone call from Elizabeth Solkhon who was working as a freelance for the local radio station. She asked me if she could come and interview me and make a tape for a future broadcast. We hit it off from the start of what, for me, has proved a wonderful friendship. Actually we made several broadcasts and as a result of these, Richard Binstead, who was on the staff of the local *Evening Argus*, contacted me and asked me if I would do some reviewing of classical music for his paper. After this, for a number of years, I wrote the criticisms of the Brighton and Hove Philharmonic concerts, and also reviewed certain musical events for the annual Brighton Festival and occasional operatic performances at Glyndebourne. I was of course delighted and as I was given two complimentary tickets for these occasions I always offered a seat to Elizabeth Solkhon – 'Liz' as I now knew her, and she became my constant companion and helped me greatly with her advice. She had sung professionally under the name of Elizabeth Hutchings and was also the press officer for the Brighton Youth Orchestra, and I always valued her opinion when writing my reviews.

I had been letting rooms to students ever since I moved to Brighton and had a second room plus kitchen and toilet built in the roof. What I now had was virtually a self-contained flat and it was occupied by two students until 1983. The previous year I had invited an old friend, Michael Murdon from the Liverpool Opera Circle, to spend a week's holiday with me and the following year in September 1983 he took early retirement and moved down to Brighton to join me, occupying the spare bedroom and sharing expenses with me. When the students left, I rented the upstairs flat for a time to a petty officer in the Merchant Navy and later to an Indian professor and his wife. He was lecturing at Sussex University and they proved to be very good tenants. By the time they left to return to India in late 1985 it was obvious that my Labrador, Mimi, was ageing very quickly. She found it difficult to walk up the few steps to the rear garden or to jump into the car, and her hearing deteriorated rapidly.

The end came rather suddenly. She had been reasonably well one day, and I had invited some friends to dinner. Most exceptionally Mimi was very restless and went into the garden and tried to push her way through a fence into a neighbour's property. Eventually I brought her back and when I went to bed she slept for a while in her basket but in the early hours of the morning she became very distressed and could not stand on her hind legs. There was nothing for it but to comfort her as best I could and send for the vet. Mimi was soon at peace and Michael and I paid her a tearful farewell. She had been a lovely, gentle companion and we both adored her. She has a permanent place in our memories.

I had been rather worried by the number of burglaries in the area, mainly by petty thieves and vandals. I was afraid someone would break in, and knowing nothing about the value of my records, pull them off their shelves, looking for money or valuables and stamp on the discs for the sheer love of wanton destruction. I therefore decided to sell gradually my major rarities after having copied them on tape. I also began to collect LPs of the great artists of the past, and so I was able to part with most of my collection without too much regret, although of course I still bought the occasional 78 and could never resist going to the local flea markets on my holidays abroad.

At about the same time – June 1986 – I felt that I would like to move to a smaller property, nearer the shops and possibly in Hove where the ground was fairly flat. I liked my garden but hated looking after it, and the gardener who came for two mornings a week was expensive and not very satisfactory. Now that Mimi had gone a really nice flat seemed the answer and in June 1986 I decided to move and asked Michael if he would be prepared to come with me. He agreed and after a good deal of flat hunting we found one which seemed ideal. It was in the Drive in Hove and consisted of two bedrooms one of which was very large while the other was big enough to accommodate comfortably a double bed. Both had well-equipped built-in cupboards while the living-room was a good size with a balcony overlooking the Drive. The kitchen and bathroom were both quite large but needed updating, and there was a separate toilet. The flat was on the seventh floor of a large block and from the kitchen window there was a splendid view of Grand Avenue – a wide thoroughfare leading to the sea which was clearly visible.

I sold the bungalow for a good price and had a nice margin of profit after buying the flat. This enabled me to modernize the bathroom toilet and kitchen at a total cost of some £15,000. Otherwise the flat was in immaculate condition and remained so for the next six years.

I suggested that Michael should have the larger bedroom to accommodate his very large collection of records and reference books and he made it into a very comfortable bed-sitting room with his own hi-fi apparatus, so that when I entertained my bridge-playing friends he could retire to his own room to read or play records!

I was very keen to revisit Venice and to meet an ex-pupil of mine who was now studying in the city with an Italian maestro. Michael was also anxious to pay his first visit there and we spent a wonderful week visiting many places of interest in the autumn of 1986 before returning home in time for Christmas, when our guests included Marjorie Hill from Liverpool.

Early in the New Year I invited Eva Turner to come down for lunch and to see the new flat and we had a very pleasant time with some of her old musical friends who now lived in Hove. Among them were Gwen Catley and her husband, Michael Langdon and his wife, and Loreley Dyer. Unfortunately, Eva's long-standing companion, Ann Ridyard, was unable to come. She had recently had a severe stroke and was in a nursing home.

1987 was a year of holidays! Number one was in April when we took a coach tour to Lugano, stopping at Valenciennes and in the Black Forest on the way down, staying for four nights in Lugano, and returning home via Nancy and Peronne.

The coach was comfortable and the scenery magnificent but we found the one-night stops on the coach journey were rather unsettling, as we were having to constantly unpack and repack our suitcases.

On our return I was asked to review *La Traviata* and *Carmen* at Glyndebourne for the *Evening Argus* in May, and Liz Solkhon went with me and we discussed the performances together before I sent in my criticisms to the paper.

Holiday number two that year was a return visit to Prague in June. We stayed for a week, visiting *Dvorák*'s birthplace and attending performances of opera at the National and Smetana theatres.

Once back in England there were numerous talks to be given and I went with Liz to a number of events in the annual festival in Arundel where she was reviewing for *Music and Musicians*. Then in September I paid my annual visit to Liverpool to give a talk on Verdi to the Liverpool Opera Circle, while Michael was very happy to return to his native town and to look up a number of his old friends. Further talks followed when we returned to Brighton and then in late October we went to Bournemouth to talk to the local Bournemouth Gramophone Society on the operas of Puccini, and this was the first of what became an annual engagement, concentrating mainly on operatic subjects.

Michael and I had decided to be very extravagant and have holiday number three! We flew out to Moscow on 7 November when the Communist Party were still firmly in power. We found that many of the officials in the very busy hotel where we stayed were supremely conscious of their own importance! One woman who was responsible for theatrical bookings was particularly aggressive. I asked politely in the morning if there were any tickets available during the next two days for the Bolshoi and was told very brusquely to come back at three in the afternoon. I duly returned at the appointed time and found myself in a long queue. When I eventually reached the woman in charge she said, 'Why did you not come earlier? Why have you left it so late?' She then very grudgingly handed me two tickets for a performance of the ballet *Don Quixote*. They were in the extreme right-hand corner of the 'Gods' but at least we were able to catch an occasional bird's-eye view of the performance!

To be fair though, we met some very charming people and my particular friend Andrej, whom I had met when he came to England some 20 years earlier with a party of students, to whom I gave a talk on English music, was particularly helpful. He earns his living as an interpreter and translator and his English was perfect without a trace of an accent, and he went round with us and assisted us with our shopping.

I remember we went to the biggest record shop in Moscow and Andrej asked a young girl assistant if they had any 'historical' LPs of famous singers of the past. She replied rather offhandedly in the negative, and was obviously more interested in 'pop', but we walked round a corner and there on the counter was a whole pile of the very records I wanted, including LPs of Figner, Mei Figner, Litvinne, Erschov and of course Chaliapin!

Life was not easy for most Russians, as we found out. We went on an organized tour of Moscow, visiting Red Square and the Kremlin, and a charming lady guide asked us, when we stopped in a shopping centre, if we would buy half a dozen tins of lager for her! They were in a shop where only foreigners could make any purchase and so she asked us to help her. She handed us the money and we made the necessary transaction paying in US dollars which the guide had received in tips.

After four days in Moscow we were taken by train overnight to St Petersburg and found a much more relaxed atmosphere in this very beautiful city. We visited the Hermitage, the Winter Palace and saw an exciting performance of Tchaikosky's *The Queen of Spades* in the Mali theatre.

Upon returning to England I was very busy with talks to various societies, and one of these was the last time I had the honour of sharing the platform with Dame Eva Turner when she addressed the BBC Philharmonic Club:

Christmas itself was a very happy occasion, when Marjorie Hill and other friends joined us for the traditional lunch, which I cooked. We spent the rest of the day quietly, listening to music, hearing the Queen's speech, and of course distributing our presents!

Altogether, 1987 had been a very happy and busy year with the holiday in Russia still fresh in our minds!

1988 started off quietly with a few talks to various societies and a reasonable amount of bridge playing which I took up again after having given it up for a number of years, but undoubtedly the most interesting event of January was a visit to the Theatre Royal to see a play *A Man for all Seasons* based on the life of Sir Thomas More. The leading roles were taken by Charlton Heston and Gwen Watford. As I had known Gwen for a number of years through her husband Richard Bebb the actor and well known record collector, I went with Michael to meet her after the performance, and she introduced us to Charlton Heston who gave a magnificent portrayal of Sir Thomas More. We were both deeply impressed by his quiet dignity and gracious bearing on stage and this was equally apparent when we met him privately.

I continued reviewing the Brighton Philharmonic concerts at the Dome for the Evening Argus, and then Michael and I decided to have an early holiday in Italy, flying out to Rome on the 21 February and visiting the usual tourist attractions including of course the Sistine Chapel and the Vatican Museum. Unfortunately there were no performances at the Teatro dell'Opera during the four days we spent in Rome, but we met some English friends who live there and we were able to enjoy some excellent meals in the local trattorie. On the fifth day we left for Venice and I envied Michael his first visit there. I had already been twice before, the first time with my mother and later to meet an ex-pupil of mine who was studying singing with an Italian maestro, but I remember well my first glance of that wonderful city as we approached by boat and were entranced by our first sight of the splendid buildings lining the Grand Canal. Subsequent visits brought back memories but nothing could equal the thrill of my first view of the splendours of Venice. All too soon our four days were over and we flew back to Gatwick and arrived home on the last day of February – the 29th as it was a Leap Year.

March was a busy month with further reviews, a number of talks and a short visit to my niece Jennifer, who was practising as a solicitor in the small town of Diss in Norfolk.

Wanderlust was already in the air again and we arranged to go to Naples on the 7 April for an operatic tour which included tickets for a performance of *Puritani* at the famous San Carlo theatre. The principal singers were Cecilia Gasdia who was really excellent and Rockwell Blake, the well known American tenor who was almost inaudible in the large auditorium. His solo 'A te o cara' which should have been one of the highlights of the evening passed by insignificantly.

The week in Naples was much too short as there was so much to see in this exciting city, with journeys to Pompeii and Sorrento as added attractions. We were warned of the dangers of pickpockets and one lady in our party had her handbag snatched by a boy of about ten within twenty yards of the hotel where we were staying. The incident ended in rather an amusing way. As the boy snatched the bag it opened and the contents fell out on the pavement. The young thief ran away with the bag containing lipstick and a powder compact, while the lady was able to retrieve from the pavement her passport, a wallet containing her money and travellers' cheques. All ended fairly happily but it was a frightening episode for an elderly lady to experience.

After spending the first few weeks of 1989 quietly at home, we decided to visit Portugal and stayed in Lisbon for two weeks. A cousin of mine had married a Portuguese businessman and we contacted his family. He and his wife were most kind and took us round the countryside, visiting a number of interesting places. Unfortunately I had a heavy cold which left me with acute bronchitis and so the last half of our holiday was severely restricted.

In May we paid a visit to Prague where I met my Czech friends and visited their delightful home in Tousen, a little village about 20 miles from Prague. We returned home on the 18 May and spent the rest of the early summer fairly quietly, while I gave my usual talks to various societies and also played quite a reasonable amount of bridge.

However, early September saw us going to Lugano for a week, and while there we visited Brusino Arsizio where I had often stayed at Dame Eva Turner's villa, and then crossed the border into Italy and lunched at the Albergo al Cervo – an old favourite of ours.

We returned in mid-September, in time for me to go to Liverpool to give a talk to the Opera Circle, and then came back to Hove for a few weeks, before flying out to Florence on the 9th October!

The rest of the year we spent in Hove, and with considerable help from Michael I entertained ten guests to Christmas lunch which I cooked myself.

1990 started quietly, but our love of travel soon put an end to this, and we flew out to Malta on the 19th February, and stayed there in Sliema for two weeks. There was plenty to do and I was able to pay a return visit to Richard England, the famous architect, whom I had met many years earlier on my first visit to Malta.

We returned to Hove on 5 March and settled down, but not for long! The travel bug soon bit us again and we flew out to Bologna on 26 April and spent a very happy week there, returning to Hove on 4 May.

Two friends of mine, Mr and Mrs Peter Court, had decided to buy a house in France and they invited us to visit them in St Valéry for a short stay of five days, and we returned with the firm intention of spending the rest of the year quietly at home but the opportunity arose to return to Lugano on 12 September, and we stayed there for just five days and then returned.

However my friends in Prague tempted us once again with the promise of seats at the opera on several nights, and so we flew out for a week on 25 October. After that we settled down and I gave my usual round of talks until Christmas.

We spent the first few weeks of 1991 at home in the flat and Michael's health was a cause of some concern as he was passing blood in his urine. He saw his local doctor and then a specialist at Brighton General Hospital and it was unfortunately confirmed that he had a small but malignant growth in his bladder. However after treatment his general condition improved and we were able to take a coach holiday in March, spending four days in Vienna, then two in Budapest and finally four in Prague, where we met my Czech friends.

The rest of the early summer we stayed at home in the flat but finally on 4 September we felt we needed a change and visited Amsterdam for four days. Our last holiday in 1991 was spent in Prague, where we stayed for a week. Our Czech friends had been able to buy us seats for various operas during the week of 14 October and we arrived home with the intention of remaining in Hove for the rest of the year. Michael's general health was now causing us considerable anxiety and it was eventually decided that he would have to have his bladder completely removed. He entered the Brighton General Hospital on 11 November and remained there for a few days to convalesce before returning to the flat. Fortunately he was well enough to enjoy our usual Christmas festivities. I always invited several lonely people to Christmas lunch which I cooked myself and Michael was able to help me in serving the meal after which we relaxed and listened to the Queen's speech.

The year ended quietly, but it was obvious that Michael was far from well. However, he was very keen to visit New York, and we flew out from Gatwick on 29 March 1992, and I gave a talk to a society of record collectors while we were there. After an enjoyable week we returned home on 6 April.

I knew that Michael very much wanted to go to Sicily despite his general condition, and I felt that this might well be his last holiday, and so I arranged for us to go to Taormina on 9 May, and we spent a very happy week there.

On our return he was in no condition to go on further holidays and we spent the rest of 1992 quietly, visiting many of our friends in Brighton and Hove and enjoying car rides in rural Sussex.

By the end of the year Michael was suffering considerable pain and it became clear that his days were numbered. He was admitted to Brighton General Hospital early in February and I visited him there every day, and although he was heavily sedated he was fully conscious. Finally the matron told me that he was sleeping peacefully and that the end was near. He died on 23 February 1993.

Michael had not made a will, but he had left a large collection of records and books and I suggested that I should give the family £1,000 and keep the collection myself. They were very generous in suggesting that they would like me to keep the records and books for my lifetime and to make proviso in my will to return them to his family upon my death.

70

POSTSCRIPT

I had made many friends in Brighton and Hove and I spent a very happy Christmas at the house of Ian Weir in 1995, and we saw quite a lot of each other. Then early in 1996 Ian told me that if ever I felt unable at my age to continue living alone, he would be happy to let me share his large house with him, and after much thought I asked him if I could spend a month at his place to see how we both felt about our possible sharing. I was only too glad to give up the responsibilities of running a flat on my own, and long before the month was over I had decided that I would like to move permanently. Immediately after that I put my flat on the market, and in September I left Normandy House and moved, taking with me various pieces of furniture, my books, some precious photographs signed by famous singers, my records and my hi-fi equipment. Ian very kindly made room for everything, and I soon felt quite at home.

My flat was duly sold in January 1997 and I was delighted that it was bought by Helen Black who was very happy to move down from London.

Ian and I decided to have a small party for Christmas dinner in 1996, and after this we spent the rest of the spring and early summer fairly quietly, looking forward to a holiday in Sorrento. We invited two friends, Phyllis and Robert to join us and left for Sorrento on 4 July, arriving in Naples airport in the early afternoon. We decided to take a taxi to Sorrento and after a hair-raising journey, thanks to some dangerous driving by other motorists, we reached Sorrento in time for dinner at the Hotel Capo di Monte.

We enjoyed a relaxing fortnight at this excellent hotel with its four swimming pools, and also took a delightful cruise from Sorrento to Amalfi.

My friends were very secretive one morning and told me that they had prepared a surprise for me and that a taxi would soon be calling for us. It duly arrived and took us to the famous Hotel Vittoria where Caruso spent much of the last months of his life. To my delight and amazement my friends had previously spoken to the manager and had arranged for me to visit the suite which Caruso had occupied.

As I have already written, Caruso has always been my idol and this visit so thoughtfully arranged by my friends touched me very deeply. However, that was not the end! They had also booked a table for lunch at the Ristorante Caruso in Sorrento, where Caruso often dined, and there were autographed photographs of the great singer proudly displayed in the restaurant. This was, for me, the climax of a wonderful holiday which I shall always remember.

We returned home on 18 July and I found that Ian had arranged a really wonderful party for my 87th birthday on 23 July. Again I was told that they had arranged a special surprise for me. I was enjoying a drink before our evening meal, relaxing and reminiscing a great deal, when Phyllis announced 'May I have your attention for a minute, we have another visitor', and to my amazement and great delight she brought in Donald (now Sir Donald) Sinden, who had come down especially for the occasion. Ian and our mutual friends Robert and Phyllis had arranged it all, and had made it, for me, an unforgettable evening, the memory of which I shall always treasure.

At the moment, at my age, I am not thinking of any more holidays abroad, and am enjoying the peace and comfort of the lovely home I share with Ian, but who knows? Even at the age of 87 I still love travel!

GLOSSARY

ALBANI Dame Emma (1847–1930)
Emma Albani was born in Chambly near Montreal in Canada.
She studied in Paris with Duprez and later in Milan with
Lamperti. She made her début in *Messina* in 1869, but her real
success followed her first appearance at Covent Garden in 1872.
Her voice was a lyric soprano of beautiful quality with a
particularly brilliant upper register and great facility in
coloratura. At Covent Garden she created many characters
including Mignon, Elsa, Elisabeth, Senta and Desdemona. She
recorded for G&T in 1904 and Pathé Frères in 1905 and all her
records are major rarities.

ARDITI Luigi (1822–1903)
Italian composer and conductor. He is now remembered for his
song Il Bacio but he was a fine conductor and gave the first
London performances of Boito's *Mefistofele*, Mascagni's
Cavalleria Rusticana and Humperdinck's *Hansel and Gretel*.

BAILLIE Dame Isobel (1895–1983)
Dame Isobel had a lyric soprano voice ideally suited to oratorio.
She was the leading English concert soprano for many years and
occasionally appeared in opera, but she will always be
remembered for her interpretation of the great sacred works in
which she was unrivalled. She recorded for Columbia.

BATTISTINI Mattia (1856–1928)
Battistini was popularly known as 'La Gloria d'Italia' and was
recognised in his prime as the greatest living baritone. His voice
reached a resonant top 'A' and his technique was unsurpassed.
Massenet adapted the tenor music of Werther so that the great

73

baritone could sing the role originally written for a tenor. He recorded in 1903 for G&T and later for HMV and in 1920 made two titles for Fonotechnica in Switzerland, but it is above all his work for HMV by which he will be remembered.

BORGIOLI Dino (1891–1960)
Borgioli was a famous operatic tenor particularly admired for his performances of works by Mozart and Rossini. His voice was a lyric tenor which he used with great taste. Upon his retirement from the stage he gave many broadcast recitals and taught singing in London and one of his finest pupils was the soprano Joan Hammond. He recorded for Columbia.

BUTT Dame Clara (1873–1936)
Her only operatic performances were as Orfeo when she was a student and in 1920 when she sang the same role at Covent Garden. She was mainly a concert singer with a superb contralto voice of immense power and wide range. Later in life her technique was faulty with a distinct break between the lower notes of her chest register and her upper range, and she devoted far too much time to singing second rate ballads which were unworthy of her talents. She recorded for HMV and later for Columbia.

CALVE Emma (1858–1942)
Calvé was a French soprano who had a very great career in the major opera houses of the world. Her *Carmen* was probably her greatest role, but she could sing lyric soprano roles like Marguérite in Gounod's *Faust* and she also had great fluency in her coloratura singing. She recorded for International Zonophone, G&T, Victor and finally for Pathé Frères.

CARUSO Enrico (1873–1921)
Caruso is so well known that biographical details are really superfluous. He made his début in Naples in 1895 and sang his last performance in New York in 1920. He recorded for G&T in 1902 on single sided red label records and in 1903 he made seven titles for International Zonophone and three for Pathé Frères.

From 1904 onwards he was an exclusive Victor artist, and his records were issued in Europe by HMV, the sister company of Victor.

CHALIAPIN Fedor (1873–1938)
Chaliapin was already world famous when he made the first celebrity records for G&T in 1901. He had made a début in St. Petersburg in 1894 and like Caruso, his career is so well known that there is little to add. He recorded exclusively for the Gramophone Company and his later records are still easily obtainable.

DE RESZKE Jean (1850–1925)
Jean de Reszke was the undisputed king of tenors following his début in 1884. He retired in 1902 and was a celebrated teacher for many years. He made tests for the Fonotipia company in Paris in 1905, but was dissatisfied with the results and forbad their publication. A few private cylinder recordings were made in New York in 1901–2 but again they were only made privately and only exist in transcriptions made from the original cylinders which were recorded from live performances at the Metropolitan Opera and give little idea of his voice.

DE RESZKE Edouard (1853–1917)
Edouard de Reszke was a bass and was the brother of Jean. He also had a highly successful career and recorded 3 titles for Columbia in 1903. They give some idea of the artist and are very rare in their original form issued with a red and gold label for a few months and a little later with black and silver labels. They are the only commercially recorded discs of the two brothers.

DESTINN Emmy (1873–1930)
Destinn or Destinnova as she is known in her native Czecho-Slovakia was one of the great operatic stars of the first two decades of the twentieth century. She was essentially a lyric soprano but was able to undertake certain heavy dramatic roles like Salome in Richard Strauss's opera of that name. It is however as Butterfly that she will always be remembered. She recorded

prolifically for G&T, HMV, Odeon and Columbia.

DE LUCA Guiseppe (1876–1950)
In an age of many great baritones De Luca was one of the very finest. He was particularly renowned for his singing of the great Verdi baritone roles. He also created the character of Sharpless in Puccini's *Madama Butterfly* and sang for over 30 years at the Metropolitan Opera New York. He recorded for G&T, Fonotipia and then almost exclusively for Victor.

DE LUCIA Fernando (1860–1925)
De Lucia was renowned for his mastery of bel canto and was a great favourite at Covent Garden where he made his début in 1887. He was idolised by the opera lovers of Naples and in his later years was a celebrated teacher. He recorded for G&T, Fonotipia and Fonodisc.

EAMES Emma (1865–1952)
Emma Eames was a pupil of Mathilde Marchesi and made a brilliant début in Paris as Juliette, a role for which Gounod coached her. She was very successful for some seasons at Covent Garden, where she threatened to rival Melba in popularity, but did not appear there after 1901. She made her début at the Metropolitan Opera New York also in 1891 and sang there until her retirement in 1911. She recorded exclusively for Victor and her discs were issued in Great Britain by the Gramophone Company.

ERSHOV Ivan (1867–1943)
Ershov was very highly esteemed in his native Russia and was particularly famous for his Wagnerian interpretations. He recorded in 1903 for G&T and Columbia and his very rare records are among the collectors' prizes.

GALLI-CURCI Amelita (1882–1963)
Galli-Curci first recorded in 1916 after a sensational début in Chicago and her records made exclusively for Victor were of extraordinary beauty. She confined her operatic appearances after

1916 almost entirely to America, but gave concert tours in England from 1924 to 1935. Her records, issued in Great Britain on the HMV Celebrity label, are fairly common even today on dealers' lists.

HYDE Walter (1875–1951)
Walter Hyde was particularly successful in Wagnerian roles which he sang at Covent Garden from 1908 until 1923. He was the first English Parsifal and later became a celebrated teacher, with whom the writer of these notes studied. He recorded for Odeon and later for HMV.

LASSALLE Jean (1847–1909)
Jean Lassalle made his début at the Opéra in Paris as William Tell in 1872 and upon the retirement of Jean-Baptiste Faure in 1878 he became the leading baritone in this theatre for twenty years. He created leading roles in Reyer's *Sigurd*, Saint-Saens' *Henry VII* and Paladilhe's *La Patrie* and was particularly famous for his Hans Sachs in Wagner's *Die Meistersinger*. He recorded some cylinders for Pathé in 1903 and some discs for Odeon in 1904-5 and they are greatly prized by collectors.

LITVINNE Félia (1861–1936)
Félia Litvinne was a pupil of Pauline Viardot-Garcia and was acknowledged as one of the greatest dramatic sopranos of her generation. She was acclaimed at Covent Garden, the Metropolitan Opera New York and in Paris and was the first Isolde to sing the role in France. She retired from opera in 1916 but continued to sing at concerts until 1924, after which she became a celebrated teacher. Among her famous pupils were Nina Koshetz and Germaine Lubin. She recorded for G&T, Fonotipia, Odeon and Pathé.

MARCHESI Blanche (1863–1940)
Blanche Marchesi was the daughter of the famous teacher Mathilde Marchesi and became a successful singer, although her voice was not outstanding. However her great intelligence and her faultless technique enabled her to have a very successful

career and she became a famous teacher in later life. The writer of these notes studied with her and among her famous pupils were Frances Alda, Muriel Brunskill and Astra Desmond. She recorded a few records for G&T in 1906, and then in the mid-thirties, when she was over seventy, she made some electrically recorded discs which are superb and highly valued among collectors.

MELBA Dame Nellie (1861–1931)

Melba was an Australian named Helen Porter Mitchell and she studied with an Italian teacher in Melbourne without outstanding success, but she asked her father, who was a prosperous builder in Melbourne, to finance her for a year if she came to Europe. She studied with Mathilde Marchesi and after a successful début in Brussels, she made her first appearance at Covent Garden in 1888. Within a year she created a sensation as Juliette and for the next thirty eight years she sang at Covent Garden where she became the prima donna assoluta, and for many years her word there was law.

She had a voice of wonderful purity and in her younger days her coloratura singing was unsurpassed in its brilliance and ease.

She was finally persuaded to make records for G&T in 1904. They were all single sided and the 12" discs were priced at one guinea and the 10" ones at twelve shillings and six pence. She continued to record exclusively for the Gramophone Company and its American sister Victor throughout her long career and finally made a few electric recordings after her farewell at Covent Garden in 1926.

MAUREL Victor (1848–1923)

Maurel was a great singing actor although his voice was not an outstanding one. He used it however with matchless skill and was a great favourite in Europe and America. Because of his superb dramatic gifts Verdi chose him to create the role of Iago in his *Otello* and also the title role in *Falstaff*. He recorded first for G&T in 1903 and then for Fonotipia in 1905 and after a long career he settled as a teacher in New York until his death in 1923.

78

McCORMACK John (1884–1943)
In his early years McCormack had a lyric tenor voice of great beauty, and he used his voice with wonderful artistry. His recording of 'Il mio tesoro' from Mozart's *Don Giovanni* is still unsurpassed. By the beginning of the first world war he had decided to concentrate on concert singing for he knew he was a poor actor on the stage. Among his later acoustic records there is a superb disc of 'O sleep why dost thou leave me' from Handel's *Semele*, and of course his Irish ballads are inimitable. He recorded on cylinders, then for G&T, Odeon and finally for HMV and Victor.

NASH Heddle (1896–1962)
Heddle Nash studied in Italy with the famous tenor Giuseppe Borgatti, and upon his return to England he quickly made a great name for himself as an excellent operatic artist and as an outstanding interpreter of Handel's *Messiah* and other sacred works. He recorded exclusively for Columbia.

NICHOLS Agnes (1877–1959)
Agnes Nichols was for some years the leading British dramatic soprano. She was the wife of the conductor Sir Hamilton Harty. She sang Sieglinde and Brunhilde in the English version of *The Ring* at Covent Garden under the great Hans Richter in 1908 and was also celebrated for her Donna Elvira in Mozart's *Don Giovanni*. She recorded for HMV in 1908–9.

NILSSON Christine (1843–1921)
Christine Nilsson was recognised as one of the greatest sopranos of the second half of the nineteenth century. Her voice was of lovely bird-like quality combined with brilliance and she was the creator of the role of Ophélie in Amboise Thomas's *Hamlet* in Paris in 1868. She was a very beautiful woman and possessed great personal charm. She made no records.

PATTI Adelina (1843–1919)
Patti was a coloratura soprano who dominated the operatic stage almost from the time of her début in 1859 until her retirement in

the first years of this century. Her great fame was due to her superb voice which had a range of from C to F in altissimo and was amazingly flexible when she was in her prime. She was known as 'The Queen of Song' and was unrivalled in her time. She sang for twenty five successive seasons at Covent Garden and was also heard in many lyric soprano roles including Marguérite in Gounod's *Faust*, Leonora in Verdi's *Il Trovatore* and even Aida in his opera of that name.

She was eventually persuaded to record in 1905 when past her prime and although the voice had lost its very highest notes, the quality remained very beautiful, and certain of her discs contain some exquisite singing. She recorded only for G&T in 1905 and 1906 and insisted that the recordings should take place at her castle at Craig y nos in Wales.

PEARS Peter (1910–1986)
Although Peter Pears had a voice of limited appeal, he was unique in his interpretation of the works of his friend Benjamin Britten. He created the role of Peter Grimes in the opera of that name and gave many recitals where his great musical intelligence and his pleasing personality were shown at their best. He recorded for HMV and Decca.

PINZA Ezio (1892–1957)
Ezio Pinza was one of the greatest operatic personalities of his day. His voice was really a basso-cantante with sufficient range for him to sing certain baritone roles like Don Giovanni in Mozart's opera. His superb appearance made him particularly suitable for many of the roles in which he was unsurpassed. When he retired from the operatic stage he appeared in 1949 in *South Pacific* with tremendous acclaim. He recorded for Victor and HMV in his prime and a little later for Columbia.

PONS Lily (1904–1976)
Lily Pons made her début as Lakmé in the opera of that name and sang for a few years in the French provinces where she was heard by the tenor Giovanni Zenatello. He recommended her to Gatti-Cassaza at the Metropolitan Opera New York where she made her

début as Lucia in 1931 with tremendous success. She sang a delightful Rosina in Rossini's *Il Barbiere di Siviglia* at Covent Garden in 1935 and continued to sing at the Met until 1959. She recorded originally for Odeon and later for Victor and Columbia.

PLANÇON Polydor (1854–1914)
Plançon possessed a genuine basso-profundo voice of lovely quality, smooth and effortless throughout its wide range. In addition he had acquired a technical mastery which enabled him to sing rapid scale passages and trills which were the envy of many sopranos. He was a great favourite at Covent Garden, the Metropolitan Opera New York and of course in Paris. He recorded for G&T and International Zonophone and later for Victor and all his records are highly prized by collectors. He recorded his great favourite the 'Air du Tambour-Major' from *Le Caïd* by Thomas four times and he sings it with inimitable verve and gallic swagger!

TETRAZZINI Luisa (1871–1940)
Tetrazzini was already famous in South America and Russia when she first came quite unheralded to Covent Garden in November 1907. She was an immediate and overwhelming success and became a great favourite and was equally successful in America. Her coloratura technique was quite amazing and her voice had a power and dazzling brilliance in its upper range. She recorded for Zonophone in the U.S.A. in 1905 and from 1907 onwards for HMV and Victor. Her London recordings of 1909 and 1910 are probably her finest and show a technical ability and ease in the most difficult florid passages.

TEYTE Dame Maggie (1888–1976)
Maggie Teyte studied briefly in London and then in Paris with Jean de Reszke. She made her début in Monte Carlo as Zerlina in Mozart's *Don Giovanni* and became a close friend of Debussy with whom she studied the role of Mélisande. She was a superb interpreter of the French repertoire and gave many recitals of the works of Debussy, Hahn, Duparc and Chausson and other French composers. In later life she taught in London. She recorded one

81

solo for the Gramophone Company in 1908 , then for Columbia and Decca and then produced an album for a famous London store. Finally HMV re-recorded many of her discs on long playing records and issued an album with the title 'L'exquise Maggie Teyte'.

TURNER Dame Eva (1892–1990)
Dame Eva joined the chorus of the Carl Rosa Opera Company in 1916 and shortly afterwards made her début as a soprano as the Page in Wagner's *Tannhäuser.* She remained with the Carl Rosa company until 1924 when she was auditioned by Toscanini who chose her to make her début at La Scala Milan as Freia in Wagner's *Das Rheingold.* She soon became famous in Italy and was particularly acclaimed for her singing of the title role in Puccini's *Turandot.* Alfano, who completed the score after Puccini's death, considered her the ideal Turandot. She sang with great success at Covent Garden from 1928 until 1948 when she became a famous teacher until her death in 1990. She recorded for Columbia and later HMV released a CD of some of her discs and also included some unpublished live recordings of performances of *Turandot* at Covent Garden.